Flight with Weighted Wings

A MEMOIR

by
Dr. Johanna O'Flaherty
and
Laurie R. Becker

ISBN: 978-1-66785-428-1 (print)
ISBN: 978-1-66785-429-8 (eBook)

Testimonials

"Dr. Johanna O'Flaherty's rich memoir reads like a good novel I didn't want to put down, even the epilogue. She weaves her life lessons through the historical lens of aviation, addiction, recovery, and, of course, her Irish family with all its pain, passion and trauma."

   —Cherlyne Short Majors, PhD
   Behavioral Health Consultant

"This is a beautifully written tale of this most fascinating woman's life lessons. Dr. O'Flaherty makes sense out of a complex topic and weaves in her colorful personal experiences, trials, and tribulations."

   —Mel Pohl, MD, DFASAM
   Senior Medical Consultant
   The Pointe Malibu Recovery Center

"Through the terror of a frightened but intuitive little girl to the calm wisdom of a seasoned addictions counselor and trauma therapist, Dr. Johanna O'Flaherty takes us along on her personal journey through her life . . . a riveting journey of a woman who worked hard to avoid facing the traumas in her life only to recognize later that those very traumatic experiences gave her everything she needed to make a huge difference in the lives of so many traumatized people. Partly poetic, partly clinical, and partly inspirational throughout, *Flight With Weighted Wings* is masterful and magnificent."

   —Jeffrey T. Mitchell, PhD, CCISM
   Clinical Professor of Emergency Health Services
   University of Maryland Baltimore County
   Co-Founder and past president of the International
   Critical Incident Stress Foundation

"A brilliant and poetically written memoir . . . captivating the reader with her romantic transgressions, along with her accomplishments in academia, in which she earns a Doctorate in Psychology. As a psychologist, she has been called upon to handle the aftermath of some of the most catastrophic and egregious events with mass casualties in recent history. Confronting the pain and grief of others forces her to look at the trauma in her own life. As you experience the author's transformation, you soon feel that transformation within yourself. A must-read for anyone trying to overcome the impact of trauma in their life."

  —Sharon Dunn
  American Airlines FA
  EAP and Critical Incident Rep

"Masterful. Dr. Johanna O'Flaherty is not only an accomplished psychologist, trailblazer, instructor, and mentor in the fields of critical incidents and trauma for airlines and first and last responders, but now has proven herself to be a skillful writer. *Flight with Weighted Wings* details her metamorphosis from a humble background in Ireland to being considered one of the top trauma experts in the industry. It was my pleasure to work side-by-side with Johanna in the aftermath of TWA Flight 800, which exploded over Long Island Sound in 1996. This manuscript grasps the reader at a visceral level as O'Flaherty takes us through her myriad experiences. This book is filled with anecdotes. It's a great read!"

  —Captain Greg Arikian, American Airlines (retired)
  Accident Investigator

"A stunningly articulate, breathtakingly descriptive, and truly interesting behind-the-scenes journey on multiple levels. From traumatic events only a participant can know and understand, to a soul journey as she integrates her experiences to provide the reader with valuable information, Dr. O'Flaherty has not only changed their vision of themselves but also the world around them. The experience is enthralling, energizing, and empowering. In short,

'Flight with Weighted Wings' is a fast read and the most important book that you will want all of your friends to read."

　—Ellyn Kravette, LSW, CASAC, CEAP

"When aircraft disasters hit the headlines, Dr. Johanna O'Flaherty was often already on the scene providing psychological support. She became today's aviation trauma and grief specialist through her efforts following Pan Am 103's explosion over Lockerbie, TWA Flight 800's demise off the shores of Long Island, and American Airlines calling her after four jetliners became terrorists' weapons during 9/11. Mass fatality shootings are another horror that most of us don't want to even think about, but Dr. O'Flaherty gets the call to counsel those directly affected, from first to last responders. Now her reflections and insight are here in her memoir. Let her take you where most hope never to have to go."

　—Mark Berry
　　Airline Pilot and author of 13,760 Feet, A TWA Flight
　　800 Memoir

"*Flight with Weighted Wings* is a must-read. A story of heritage, history, vocation and wisdom, written with courage, compassion, and devotion to spiritual truth."

　—Beata Lundeen
　　Spiritual direction provider at several treatment centers,
　　with 40 years of nursing experience in the field of
　　addiction and mental health; interventionist, business
　　development strategist and chief experience officer

"This is an enthralling memoir. It covers the wide-ranging life experiences needed to develop wisdom in a true leader. These events, from the ravages of intergenerational family trauma in the south of Ireland to working for the most prestigious airline during the "jet set" years to her development of expertise in crisis management, have all led to an unforeseen and unique set of skills. Dr. O'Flaherty has gone on to apply those skills on the ground in the immediate aftermath of events such as airline disasters and the terrorist attacks of 9/11 and through community outreach after mass casualties caused by gun violence. The substance of this memoir is best described by a quote from Lao Tzu: 'The leader is best when people barely know he exists . . . when his work is done, his aim fulfilled, they will say: we did it ourselves.'"

—Michael O'Malley
MB, BCh, BAO, CCFP, FCFP
Doctor of Family Medicine, specialty in addiction
medicine, recipient of a lifelong Fellowship in the
College of Family Physicians of Canada

"In the opening pages of Dr. Johanna O'Flaherty's memoir, she creates a haunting visual of growing up and surviving in a small village in County Kerry in the south of Ireland. As an Irish immigrant, I related. Beautifully written in a style peculiar to Irish literary giants, creating a patchwork of dark beginnings, then morphing into a life of brilliant creativity, successes and skyrocketing achievement. What is most interesting as well as entertaining is her candor about her love life with significant men, marrying only once, recognizing the gift of self, the power of womanhood. *Flight with Weighed Wings* is an emotional and scholarly read for all of us isolated, filled with fear, longing and praying for an end to the relentless conflicts of a pandemic and a nation riddled with political conflict."

—Estelle Shanley
(While a reporter for *The Lowell Sun*, Shanley was the
first woman to enter the locker room of the Boston Red
Sox days following the US Supreme Court edict lifting
the ban against females entering those hallowed halls.)

Flight with Weighted Wings is the remarkable story of Dr. Johanna O'Flaherty's life, which intersected with so many interesting and important moments in modern history. Johanna's writing flows and reads easily in a wonderful storytelling style, and her captivating personal account spans a fascinating era. From her bleak childhood to her unforeseen launch into the exciting and glamorous world of the Mad Men 1960s and '70s international jet-set as a Pan Am stewardess and cover girl, to her struggle with alcoholism and post-traumatic stress disorder, she turned it all around and became a nationally renowned specialist in addiction recovery and trauma counseling. She has trained hundreds of healthcare and disaster responders, and her work has made a deep and lasting impact on providers and patients alike. Johanna holds back nothing in sharing her own personal tragedies, and her memorial to a lost family member is particularly touching and poignant. She weaves her own family's recent heartbreak into a message of hope and recovery while not sugarcoating anything about the unknown future for any of us or our own loved ones. *Flight with Weighted Wings* is also an insightful and useful overview of the field of trauma treatment, delving into professional topics with extensive discussions including current experimental treatment for PTSD, the long-lasting scars of adverse childhood experiences, the genetic influences of cultural trauma, and the scientific validity of 12 Step Recovery programs. I highly recommend this book to anyone who has experienced trauma or struggled with chemical dependencies in their own life, and to any professional in the field of mental health or addiction treatment.

—Glenn P. Matney, MD, FASAM, DABPM,
DABAM, DABP
Board-Certified in Pediatrics and Addiction Medicine

"Like Dr. O'Flaherty herself, this sophisticated, gracious story packs a lot: a personal memoir, history of aviation, veritable who's who of the 70s and 80s, and compact training manual for recovery and disaster preparedness. But, most importantly, it does this while conveying a message of hope and once again demonstrating the true miracle of recovery. A frightened yet ambitious little girl from the verdant isle of Ireland, who experienced the traumas of a life well-lived, has something left to give others, as she does in great measure. She's easy to know, open to living all that life has to offer and connects with the reader on a deep, personal, and emotional level. You will see yourself in her every memory and want what she has been able to accumulate through honesty, openness, and a willingness to connect on a feelings level."

 —Andrea G Barthwell, MD, FASAM
  Medical Director, Encounter Medical Group
  Founder and CEO of Two Dreams recovery facilities

Dedication

In loving memory of my parents, Molly Bowler and Tom Sullivan, for the gift of my life. Learning to live it was mine alone to accomplish.

To my beloved sisters, Maureen, Bridget, Eileen, Kathleen, and brother, Patrick, whose love and acceptance have shaped me from the very beginning and saved me a million times since.

To Ireland, the land of our birth, in all its tragic, complex, and enduring beauty. Just like life itself.

And in memory of my beloved grandniece, Amelia Bambridge. The sea gives; the sea takes away, sometimes in heart-wrenching, unequal measure. For Amelia, forever in our hearts 1998–2019.

Table of Contents

Foreword

It is my pleasure and privilege to write some thoughts about my friend, Johanna O'Flaherty, for her new book *Flight with Weighted Wings*. It is a beautifully written and amazing story that I'm sure will be swept up on its own wings and taken to teach, guide, and enlighten people.

This is a story not only about Johanna's personal journey but also about the function of trauma as it relates to alcohol and drug addiction as well as other afflictions of body and soul. Hers is a truly amazing story, with her position as vice president of the Betty Ford Treatment Center, her mission as a trauma healer, and her work with first and last responders and family members of those lost in major airline crashes and terrorism. Johanna was there when an on-board bomb blew up a plane over Lockerbie, Scotland, when TWA Flight #800 exploded over Long Island Sound, and in the immediate aftermath of the 9/11 attacks in New York. She has led a remarkable life, especially for a woman who immigrated from the poorest outpost of small village life marked by poverty and domestic violence.

My relationship with Johanna O'Flaherty began in 1978 when we both found a recovery program in New York City. From those days to this one, I have benefited from Johanna's insight, clarity, and friendship. We found many similarities in our lives and careers. In some ways, both of our professional lives were composites of the times we came up in. We both had startling stories of professional journeys and our drinking, stories that would make people laugh out loud and weep at the close calls, death-defying incidents, and the remarkable miracles that we shared. And of course, when Johanna told her stories, one was additionally charmed and delighted with the accent of this beautiful, Irish lass. We became instant friends.

At the time we first met, Johanna was a flight attendant with Pan Am and told me they were on the verge of firing her because of her drinking. That very same year, my own drinking had practically shredded my career as a musician and performer. Both of us had climbed to pinnacles of success, and we had both been sliding down the heights due to our drinking.

In those days, Pan Am did not have an EAP (Employee Assistance Program). In 1981, Johanna went back to school and soon earned a Masters and PhD in psychology, with subspecialties in chemical dependency, counseling, and crisis psychology. She then started the first corporate-sanctioned EAP at Pan Am in 1986. Her future in healing trauma would be an outgrowth of her own childhood, her studies, her own humanity and hard-won sobriety. My own career, which had been in tatters when we first met, began to come to life again a few years later. When we'd meet over coffee and at other gatherings, we took pleasure and pride in each other's accomplishments. We did better than survive.

Johanna and I lost touch with one another for a few years physically, although I could never forget her musical laughter, powerful presence, and loving spirit. We were both deeply engrossed in our recovery and our careers when in 2007, I found myself in Palm Desert, California, for an appearance at the McCallum Theatre. Out of the blue came a call from Johanna O'Flaherty! I had missed my friend, and now, here she was. That bright, musical voice said, "Hi, it's Johanna!" and we were right back on track. Then she told me she was at the Betty Ford Treatment Center, just three miles away. For a moment, I thought she was in treatment there, but then she said, with that old, familiar laugh in her voice, "I run the joint!" Johanna O'Flaherty was now the vice president of the Betty Ford Treatment Center.

My granddaughter, Hollis, was with me, visiting from LA. It was after six o'clock, and the business offices at the treatment center were closed. Among the acacia and pine trees softly moving in the gentle breeze, Johanna met us at the back door of the Betty Ford Center, an impressive, modern

California-style building. I introduced Hollis; there were smiles and hugs all around. Johanna held the keys to the kingdom, and we stepped inside.

"First," Johanna said, "We'll go through the children's unit to get to my office; it's on the way." She told us the unit was for children ages six to twelve, and their parents did not have to be in treatment there; the kids could come and be part of this program for children of alcoholics and drug addicts. This blew my mind. When I was growing up in the 1940s and early '50s in Los Angeles, the child of an alcoholic father, there was no such thing as Alateen or Alatot or even AA, for all we knew. We were in the dark in more ways than one.

We arrived at Johanna's office, First Lady Betty Ford's old office, replete with Johanna's pictures and personal things arranged alongside the plaques and photographs that remained of Mrs. Ford's life. Betty Ford had been a fearless proponent of sobriety, especially for women. She was a trailblazer, as was the new occupant of her office. In a way, it was a miraculous introduction to this surprising and extraordinary life that my old friend was living. Johanna's magnificent spirit and career were now—and had been for years—in the service of survivors of both chance and intentional disasters that befall human beings, here, there, and everywhere.

I learned how Johanna had come to see this need, not previously understood or fulfilled, in connecting background trauma and seemingly insurmountable, tragic losses, to the suffering of those with chemical dependencies or grave mental disorders. She had spent her life working on solutions. She had developed, among other skills, her compassionate nature, her gentle approach, her sophistication of spirit, and her basic model of keeping things simple, to come up with a system of identifying and reversing the trauma to heal the original assault. She had found a means and a way to the other side of misery. Johanna's professional life had become the very essence of service. Her own background and amazing recovery had hatched out this woman, a superwoman, a super person, as well as a gentle, communicative, and spiritual presence who had the ability to help people survive trauma, old and new, in childhood as well as adulthood.

A few years after reconnecting with her in California, I was privy to a gathering in New York where Johanna, instructing a group at Fordham University, discussed her process of unraveling trauma to address subsequent addictions. It was an experience I'll never forget. I learned a great deal about the correlation between childhood trauma and subsequent addictions and felt relieved of much of the painful impact of my own early experiences. Listening to her and learning from her that day, I was able to draw connections between my own traumatic encounters, which gave me the insight to look at and eventually break causal behaviors in my own life.

After Johanna left the Betty Ford Treatment Center, she moved to Las Vegas and was called upon to help in the fallout of the 2017 shooting outside the Mandalay Bay/MGM Hotel, where dozens of people were murdered in cold blood by Stephen Paddock. A deranged sixty-four year-old, Paddock opened fire on the crowd gathered below for a music festival. Firing from a high floor in the MGM Hotel, Paddock murdered sixty people before killing himself. Even today, Johanna continues to participate in the healing process of firefighters and police, coroners, and medical examiners, as well as with the surviving attendees and family and friends of those lost. A few days after the horrific shooting, I was in Las Vegas, performing at The Smith Center, and I met with Johanna. I was so deeply impressed with her compassion, presence of mind, and the fact that she could counsel those who were shell-shocked by the senseless attack of a man who was clearly out of his mind. Because of her trauma counseling and compassionate presence, Johanna is often called to help in such tragic situations. Hers is a true and much-needed presence, a beacon of hope in the midnight of despair.

I am so grateful that my friendship with Johanna has been renewed and refreshed in these recent years. She is a mighty example of what can happen when your life gets turned around and how healing can occur with brilliance and a clear heart and mind. A dear friend to me and a healer to so many, Johanna O'Flaherty's life and work are blessings in this world of toil and trouble. *Flight with Weighted Wings* will lift you up and give you hope. Sometimes, hope is all we need. Thank you, Johanna.

—Judy Collins
Grammy Award-winning singer, songwriter, and
social activist
New York, October 8, 2020

Introduction

It would be hubris to claim that one woman's life, my life, should stand as a representation of the human condition of any place and time. Yet, my life as an immigrant, born out of poverty and violence in post-World War II Ireland, and my convoluted journey to adulthood where my career as a psychologist and crisis management consultant all look to me now, at seventy-three, as if my story is America's story. It has not always been, and it will, blessedly, not always be. But at this moment in time, when American families and the very fabric of our country are besieged by the combined traumas of addiction and gun violence set against a backdrop of a polarized and heartbreaking shift in immigration policy, my personal story feels, to me, to be the individual manifestation of the very history we are currently living through.

History is taught through stories; the young gather at the knees of their elders and listen. The elders may not only be gathered to speak, to inform but may also be gathered to heal themselves. I am a person who often doesn't know how I feel or what I need until I write it or somehow articulate it out loud. The telling of my story is not only for your eyes but also for my understanding.

After a recent talk I gave on the correlation between multigenerational trauma and addiction, several attendees approached me and began to share aspects of their personal stories. We were united, connected at a deep, communal level in understanding the pain of traumatic childhood experiences that haunt and hinder many of us to this day. We share our personal stories of trauma to help disempower the traumatic event. Traumatic experiences leave us feeling exposed and vulnerable, stripped by circumstances beyond our personal control. Many of us suffer in silence. We are too ashamed to share our traumatic experiences with anyone because we are afraid others will judge us or use them against us somehow. Many of us don't have the words to describe what has happened to us; others have pushed the memories so far underground that words alone can't excavate the trauma.

My intention in writing this book is to share with you the story of my own trauma and the difficult, often circuitous, and self-destructive path I took to acceptance, forgiveness, and love. First, tenuously, acceptance of those who had hurt me. Acceptance, in time, unfolded into forgiveness. The longer, harder path was to learn to love me: it can be easier to love others than it is to truly love our own flawed, fragile selves. My hope is to show that suffering is not meaningless and that, in fact, the very thing that brings us pain can, in time and with care, bring us a sense of liberation and purpose. I believe that inherent in suffering is an opportunity to transform pain and consciously use the experience as a progenitor of a new way of being, a new way of living, a new way of seeing the world, and perhaps being able to help others do the same. We are all unique individuals, many of us with deep wounds from our pasts. But we do not need to let those scars define or defeat us.

The shape of my life, including my career as a clinical psychologist and specialist in community-wide crisis management, was imprinted on my psyche by traumatic events in my early childhood. My journey of self-exploration, learning, and deeply knowing myself required and still requires years of reflection and personal reckoning. Looking back at my formative years and experiences, my travels in search of spiritual meaning and comfort, and the arduous route to recovery from alcoholism, I know that all these elements in time formed my perspective, my work, and my very soul. While my life was filled with poor decisions and bad choices, my experiences created the tapestry of Me. Colored in hues dark and brooding alongside bright tones of lightness and hope, all threads twist and intertwine. I can no sooner disentangle this complicated tapestry now than I can predict its completion.

As a psychologist, I've dedicated my life's work to educating professionals and the general public about the correlation between trauma and subsequent alcohol and other drug addictions. I've spent more than three decades working with those in substance recovery and the same number of years working with those traumatized by the sudden loss of loved ones in airline disasters and terrorist attacks. As this book was being written, I was working with the first and last responders of the worst gun-related mass murder in our country's history. Through all of it, I have come to believe that whether born of a spontaneous, hideous event that leaves lives shattered or the culmination of a childhood splintered by violence, neglect, and abuse, those exposed will find themselves at the intersection of trauma and debilitating loss. To cross to safety, we must surrender what we've been hanging onto; we must loosen the grip on what we thought was a safety rope but which is, instead, the noose. Crossing over can feel like a leap of faith, the last available option, like entering a cresting river only because the entire town behind you is on fire. The river can appear raging and unpredictable and, at other times, calm and purposeful in its destination. Each of us steps into the river only when we're ready, when we become aware that standing on dry ground is the more dangerous place.

I've written this book not out of despair but out of hope. Hope that transformation is possible. Hope that with hard work and fully engaged, informed help, the aftershocks of trauma will not contaminate our loved ones. Hope that trauma can be contained, like a wildfire, by digging trenches, clearing vegetation, and wetting the perimeter. Hope that we, as professionals, as members of a family, community, and society, as members of humanity, can and will do well by those in pain and by our own wounded selves.

Having long ago stepped into the river of healing myself, I know the only way out is by moving forward while delving deeper. The reclamation of our very lives depends on it.

—Johanna O'Flaherty
Autumn 2020

The process of putting the thing you value most in the world out for the assessment of strangers is a confidence-shaking business even in the best of times.
—Ann Patchett, *Truth and Beauty*

Chapter I: Mind the Face

If you cannot get rid of the family skeleton, you may as well make it dance.

—George Bernard Shaw

In the shadows of Ireland's two tallest mountains and along the shores of the Luane River stands the historic town of Killorglin ("Orgla's Church"), population just under 2100, in the Province of Munster, County of Kerry. Killorglin was my birthplace. My family owned a small farm just outside of town, and our home had a magnificent view of the Irish Sea. Darkness lurked beneath and beside this pastoral beauty.

A stone's throw from our farm, Carrauntoohil is the isle's tallest mountain. It's the central peak in the MacGillycuddy's Reeks range and stands proudly over Killorglin at approximately 3,400 feet. If you were standing at the summit on a clear day, which you could accomplish without specialized climbing equipment, you would have an 80-mile view in every direction. You would be looking all the way to Galway Bay to the north and Bantry Bay to the south.

A 40-minute drive from Killorglin, Mount Brandon, the isle's second highest peak, stands just over 3,100 feet. Though shorter in stature than its big brother Carrantuohill, Brandon is the more revered of the two peaks, as it is the culmination of the Christian pilgrimage trail known as Cosán na Naomh ("The Saints Road"), which is thought to have originated in pre-Christian times. Small white crosses mark the path to the summit, and a large metal cross stands sentry at the apex. Yet not all of its history is blessed. Over a span of only three years, from 1940 to 1943, and just a few years prior to my birth, four airplanes crashed on or near Mount Brandon. Only now, in retrospect, does this strike me as prophetic. There was no foresight at the time that my first career would be as a commercial flight attendant; there was no way to know that I'd make a name for myself years later as a specialist in airline disaster crisis management.

As a child, these two formidable mountain peaks met my upward gaze, and the River Laune, which ran through my town, met my gaze when looking down. A rich source of salmon and trout, the river runs fourteen miles before merging with the sea. I grew up near its shoreline of 200-year-old stone and earthen embankments, originally built in the early 1800s to protect the hemp farms from flooding. The hemp was used to make sail-cloth for the British Navy during Napoleon's rule. Today these embankments still protect the farms from flooding when the rising tides of the river crest the banks.

My parents each grew up about ten miles from Killorglin and married in their 20s. My father, Tom, was seven years older than my mother, Molly. He left high school before graduation, but my mother completed her studies with the equivalent of a two-year college education and an Associate of Arts degree in General Studies. Education was very important to her, and she stressed this throughout our childhoods. As we grew, she encouraged advanced studies, wanted us to have careers, and wanted her daughters to "marry up" so they, and their potential future children, would have a better life than her own. She had a head full of dreams for us.

My childhood in Ireland is framed in the 1950s, just after World War II, when the country was experiencing great hardship and poverty. I am the second to last born of six children; we were five daughters and one son. Our household was one of cramped space and chaos, a cacophony of six children, my parents, and Uncle Joe, my father's brother. We all lived together in a three-bedroom house, without the luxury of indoor plumbing, just outside the small town of Killorglin. Killorglin is in a very remote area of Ireland, and everyone in the village struggled just to get by. We were no different than our neighbors who lived off the land and the sea as farmers and fishermen. My father was both, just as his father had been before him.

My father was a hard-working man, and he provided for his large family. He was also, periodically, a hard-drinking man and, when drunk, caused havoc in our home. My brother, Patrick, the second child, was the light in my mother's eye. This didn't mean, however, that she could protect him from my father's alcoholic rages. Nor could she protect my sisters, herself, or me.

My father was not an everyday drinker; the cost of booze and the vacancy of his pockets prevented that. But when he did drink, he was consumed by rage. He became verbally and physically abusive to everyone in the household, and he was particularly harsh on my brother. Perhaps unconsciously but nonetheless "fecked–up," my father may have been taking revenge on Patrick for being my mother's favored one. With one punch, he could punish them both; a blow to Patrick for being her favorite, a blow to her for the demonstrated favoritism. He was also abusive to my older sisters and me, and I witnessed him beating them and my mother on several occasions. And yet, while his behavior could be brutal and erratic, my father was a sensitive and spiritual man. He read the Bible and prayed daily, which is uncommon for an Irish Catholic. This paradox of character was confusing for a child and created an unstable, frightening home life. It would be many years later, when I became a clinical psychologist and recovering alcoholic myself, that I would understand his mercurial behavior.

My earliest memory of my father's abuse took place when I was five years old. I witnessed him beating one of my sisters, who was only nine or ten at the time; he was striking her repeatedly with the buckle end of a belt. Intimidated and afraid to intervene, frightened that he'd turn his rage on her yet again, my mother sat by the fire, occasionally glancing up to issue the only directive she could muster. While unable to insert herself between her drunken husband and helpless young daughter, my mother was nearly mute. All she could offer by way of protection was to quietly repeat, "Mind her face; mind her face, Tom." Was this cultural collaboration between the two of them, sanctioned action that was perfectly acceptable if my sister's face was left unscarred? The irrationality and meekness of asking an enraged man to "mind her face" as he beats a young girl with a belt are incomprehensible to me now, and yet, when I imagine standing in my mother's shoes, also somewhat understandable. My mother feared my father's drunken behavior; she tried everything within her capacity to shelter us all from his demonic outbursts. For her time, my mother was highly educated, and she was not passive; she was a strong woman in many ways. She was loving and nurturing when time allowed, but raising six children, managing the small farm we called home, and coping with my father's drinking and temperament didn't leave her with much in the way of personal resources. Perhaps her feeble request was all she had, a dull tool that would neither end the beating nor exacerbate his anger. If she could stay safe herself while keeping her daughter's potential injuries invisible to others, well, maybe that was as good as she could get.

As abhorrent as this behavior is to us now, it was accepted as a cultural norm in 1950s Ireland. Not only were children beaten at home, but they were also beaten in school by their teachers and emotionally abused by the clergy. Women who approached the priest for marital counseling were essentially told, "You made your bed. Now you need to lay in it." Women were not given any practical advice on how to protect themselves or their children from abuse. Basically, there was no safe place. The beatings continued throughout my childhood; we all were overly familiar with the raw metal bite of my father's belt.

There were better, kinder times, too. I have fond memories of my father, like the times he told us nighttime ghost stories, making us laugh and scream simultaneously. And I remember his reverence, his dedication to God and His teachings. In reading the Bible and reciting his daily prayers, I believe he thought he was a good Catholic, a good husband, father, and provider. But when he drank, usually with our neighbors in the town pubs, his anger rose like a devil just paroled, and I was terrified, confused, and wanted nothing so much as I wanted to get as far away from my family as fast as I could. In 1950, that town and that country were destitute and, in large part, uneducated. Medical and psychological care was scarce, and understanding of the disease of alcoholism, which my father suffered from, was virtually non-existent. While I understand this intellectually now as a woman, this knowledge does nothing to erase the impact it had on the child I once was.

Later that same year, another frightening event occurred, which taught me that physical abuse was one way to hurt a child, and neglect was another. On my first day of school, my older sister, Maureen, walked my best friend, Margaret, and me the three miles of dirt road to the schoolhouse. I was an introverted, extremely shy child, likely rendered so by the violence I witnessed at home. I was frightened of the other children and the teachers, but Margaret was my comfort; I remember the two of us huddled together during that first morning's session. But shortly after lunch that day, Margaret became ill. Instead of being met with compassion and concern, Margaret's nausea annoyed the teacher; we felt embarrassed and ashamed in front of our classmates. The teacher instructed me and another classmate to walk Margaret home. We were three five-year-old girls trudging the three miles home alone, during which Margaret continued to vomit the entire time. Scared that I couldn't help my friend, we finally made it back to Margaret's house, where I handed her over to her mother and ran home to the shelter of my own mother. At the time, there were no telephones in our village, which is how it came to be that such young children, babies really, were tasked with bringing a very ill little girl back to her home. And how it came to be that we didn't know until the following morning, when Maureen and I stopped at Margaret's home to pick her up for school, that she had died during the night. My best friend, Margaret, a child of only five, died painfully of an untreated ruptured appendicitis. Like coastal fog sitting low on the valley floor, I felt enveloped by fear, loss, and confusion.

I can't recall how I processed this shock as a five-year-old, but I do remember how I felt. I was scared, and I was angry. There was no such thing as grief counseling back then, and there were no discussions about Margaret's death either at home or at school. The best I could do was go to church, pray, and heed the adults when they told me to "get over it." Silence, devotion, and developing a stiff upper lip were methodologies for healing grief in my home in the 1950s. This was my first exposure to death, impermanence, loss and its conjoined twin, grief. Combined with those dark lessons I was learning at the hands of my father, I sought protection from the harsh realities of life and the things I could not understand. Finding no relief in the adults who were supposed to protect me, I escaped into my imagination and would daydream for hours by the stream that flowed by our house. I'm not sure what capacity a five-year-old has to imagine being away from the only life she knew, but I didn't want to be there. Even as a child, I imagined an immediate escape not only from my family and home but from my hometown, too. If I wasn't safe at home, and Margaret wasn't safe anywhere, what other than doom did that mean for me? At five, I vowed to myself I'd find a better life elsewhere, anywhere elsewhere.

And for a while, I did. It's just that the new way of life didn't look anything like I'd imagined. Sometimes, a gift comes wrapped in heartbreak paper tied with a black ribbon, and only by looking back do we see its value and purpose. This was the gift that presented itself as a life-threatening illness that struck me six years later.

In the summer of 1958, at age eleven, I was hospitalized for three months with rheumatic fever and jaundice. Rheumatic fever is an inflammatory disease, sometimes caused by inadequately treated strep throat or scarlet fever. Medical care in Killorglin was wanting; there was one doctor in town, a woman, who made house calls in her run-down motorcar. She was called to my home when my temperature reached 105°, and I was hemorrhaging from my nose. At the time, Ireland had its fair share of sha-mans or "Cailleach" (an ancestral wise woman in Irish folklore), and our village was no exception. With us that night was our resident Cailleach from the village, Maeve, who was sage-like in her wisdom and observation. She was always brought in, or she just happened to come to the home in need, as if beckoned by a call only she could hear. I remember her looking at me and then saying to my mother, as I bled uncontrollably, "Molly, she's gone!" I vividly recall hearing her words and thinking that "being gone" would have been a gift, as my headache was unbearable. It was an intermi-nable wait of several hours before the doctor finally arrived, flustered and agitated, stating she'd gotten lost. I remember wondering how in hell she'd gotten lost in a one-road village. After her medical assessment, she arranged for me to be hospitalized, and to this day, I'm grateful; I know she saved my life. Years later, I learned the doctor's husband was an alcoholic, and I've since come to understand that living with an alcoholic can lead to confu-sion, shame, exhaustion, and other emotional consequences. No doubt the doctor's chaotic home life led to her agitation that night and the reason she couldn't find my house in such a tiny town. Over the years, my own addic-tion brought with it a softening, an acceptance, allowing what was once judgmental in me to think past the how and what of someone's impact on me and look deeper for the why. My own struggle has made me kinder.

Rheumatic fever causes muscle aches, swollen and painful knees, elbows and wrists, and high fever, but its greatest risk is to the valves of the heart, scarring them and forcing the heart to work harder. Eventually, rheu-matic fever can cause the heart to fail, as mine nearly did five decades later. My illness left me with a prolapsed mitral valve, meaning the valve between the heart's upper and lower left chambers doesn't close correctly. I denied and ignored this condition for many years until I was rushed into surgery to repair the valve after failing a cardiac stress test during a standard annual physical. Contracting rheumatic fever at eleven forced my confinement in the hospital for three months, during which I was separated from my family. I missed them dearly, even as my wish to be far away from them all, out of my house and out of my town, had come true.

I was placed in a county hospital in Killarney, about twelve miles from Killorglin. It did not have a children's ward, so I was the only child in an adult women's unit surrounded by the critically ill and dying. At that time throughout Ireland, tuberculosis (TB), better known among laypeople in those days as "consumption," ravaged the country; it was a silent terror and indiscriminate killer if left untreated. The highly contagious, airborne bacterial disease lodges in the lungs, causing sudden weight loss and breathlessness. It thrived in the poorly ventilated, thatched cottages in the countryside and in the crowded tenements of the city. In Dublin alone, more than 10,000 people died annually, more than 50% of them children.[1]

But from my hospital bed, I saw only adults dying. The women were poor and seemed very old (although they were probably only in their 30s at the time). Surrounded by the gravely ill and dying and being held captive there for three months cast an overwhelming sense of foreboding on me. I came to believe that if one managed to survive childhood, as Margaret had not, then only death awaited in adulthood. At a young and impressionable age, I saw death up close, too close, often in the bed right next to mine. I wasn't protected from the sight, sound, smell, and fear of death. I felt oddly invisible as I witnessed the priest coming onto the ward regularly to anoint the dying as the patient drew her last labored breath. And yet I was present enough to be treated to lies and dismissals by the doctors and nurses who told me daily that I'd be going home "soon, any day now" when I knew down to my core that I wasn't going anywhere, anytime soon. I became an "invisible observer" while I was there, and I developed a keen sense of intuition. And a likewise keen sense of distrust. Physicians lied; fathers beat you; mothers couldn't protect you; teachers banished you if you were unlucky enough to be sick at school before being ordered home to die. I trusted no one and felt safe nowhere.

Throughout this three-month period, my parents and siblings took turns visiting me, which literally was a labor of love since we did not own a car. Every week, they had to bicycle twenty-four miles roundtrip to see me, in rain or sleet. My father visited frequently, and I can still see the heartbreak in his eyes; this kind, loving, raging, violent, and complex man was visibly anguished that his young daughter was gravely ill. The women in the ward all liked my father; he was good-looking and could charm the birds right out of the sky when he wanted. My sister, Maureen, seventeen at the time of my confinement, was working as a waitress in a hotel not far from the hospital and was able to stop by frequently; my other siblings visited as well. My teacher came by regularly and took a particular interest in my well-being; she wanted to make sure I kept up with my studies and assignments, so I could return to grade level once I was able to go back to school. Of all who came to see me, I think the hospital visits were the hardest on my mother; the image of her panic-stricken face as she did her best to comfort me is still vivid. I think she never forgot the "Cailleach" Maeve's pronouncement and thought the prophecy of my immediate death would actualize at any moment. I still hold very fond memories of my family during my hospital stay: they made me feel loved and protected, which I had never felt at home.

During my illness, I promised God and the Blessed Virgin that if I survived, I would dedicate my life to the church by becoming a nun. I thought it was my duty to repay God for my survival. As I now reflect on that time, I believe those three months had a profound emotional and spiritual impact on me, particularly on my understanding of death. Despite being surrounded by the love of my family, the experience deeply wounded my psyche. Unconsciously, at age eleven, I developed a protective mechanism, a wall of well-defined defenses that shielded me from the maze of the adult world, which looked to be comprised of illness, violence, instability, heartbreak, fear, and death. Growing up with an abusive, alcoholic father and a mother who couldn't defend her children was one kind of trauma. Realizing that our teachers and Margaret's parents couldn't save her life was another kind. And the trauma experienced by the isolation, loneliness, and constant exposure to the dead and dying in the hospital was a trauma of yet a different sort. Bundled together, those experiences burdened and scarred that young girl, eroding the innocence of childhood. After being exposed to death at an early age, it's very hard to return to innocent play, and it's impossible to erase the experiences that became indelibly imprinted on my mind. While chronologically still a child, I'd had some of the experiences of an adult. And yet, as an invisible observer with a knack for burying my emotions while developing intuition, these traumas, these wounds, effectively provided a safe, self-protected space around me. My goal of becoming a nun was my way of not only paying off a debt to God, but I thought the convent would keep me safe from all the dangers of the adult world. And if I was safe, I could help others feel protected from the harsh realities of life, too. These were the naïve dreams of my eleven-year-old frightened self.

But there was another impetus at work, something a little scandalous that I could sanitize, or at least whitewash if I entered the convent . . . or so I thought using my childish logic. While living in that adult hospital ward, I became an acute listener and adept at intercepting the veiled conversations taking place between the women in my unit. In low, breathless tones, the women spoke a secret language among themselves about their female problems. Remember, this was the late 1950s in Ireland, where the church turned a blind eye to spousal and child abuse, where birth control was highly restricted, and where women had no voice or choice about their own bodies. The women whispered in shame about pregnancies; to be pregnant was proof you had had sex, and sex was disgraceful. It was certainly not openly discussed.

Except that here, on this death ward, it was! Enter this secret, ongoing conversation between women an exotic redhead who was admitted onto our unit. I don't know why she was there, but she shone too brightly to have been suffering from tuberculosis or any other serious disease. None of us had ever seen anything like her before, and to my preadolescent delight, this beautiful, flame-haired gypsy woman blew the lid right off the forbidden and thrilling topic. If the other women spoke from behind a hand held discreetly in front of their mouths, this wild siren shouted from a bullhorn. She openly discussed her sex life and her many lovers. She spared no detail; she left nothing to the imagination. I was eleven years old and innocent about sex. I was fascinated, and I loved her! She became my friend and co-conspirator as we whispered derogatory names for the doctors and nurses (wangers and bitches) and gossiped about everyone, sparing only those closest to death's door. My gypsy woman thought that the nuns and the nurses needed a good shag; the nuns and nurses thought that the gypsy woman was a bad influence on me. Both sides were right. The staff advised me to spend more time in the chapel in a misguided and ultimately futile attempt to reign in my newly awakened interests. Much to their dismay, I spent every moment I could with my ferocious, free-spirited friend. Her sense of liberation and devil-may-care attitude was intoxicating, especially in contrast to the stymied local women, so full of shame and repression. Her openness and lack of inhibition were potent; she represented the freedom I wanted for my future adult self. Only later did I learn that gypsy women were disproportionately vulnerable to domestic violence, at least in part due to alcoholism, and my perception of her free-spirited strength clouded when I realized her partner(s) had likely abused her. Alcoholism and physical abuse, I was learning, were rampant throughout my childhood environment regardless of how beautiful or how confident one appeared. I don't remember her name, and I don't think she was at the hospital for very long, but she left a lasting impression on me. These sixty years later, I'm still attracted to gypsy women and their lifestyle, and though I couldn't have known it at the time, my friend influenced my desire to live a life of excitement and thrill-seeking. She nurtured my curiosity about other people, other ethnicities and cultures, and other ways to live a life, especially as a woman. The picture I had of my future self as a nun was already beginning to fracture.

When I was finally discharged from the hospital, I faced a long recuperation at home. As it turned out, we all did. My illness had left a mark on the family and changed us in some fundamental ways. The doctors had recommended that during my recuperation, efforts were to be taken to keep my stress level as low as possible so my blood pressure wouldn't spike. If I were to become agitated, I'd experience shortness of breath and fainting spells. My fainting scared the "shite" out of my parents, and they and the rest of the family did their best not to fight around me. I quickly learned how to use this to my advantage: here was a doctor-ordered opportunity to mold my family into the people I thought I wanted them to be. I learned to control my environment with false swoons and manipulate my family in ways that brought peace and harmony into my home, lying for the sake, I thought, of the greater good. During that first year home from the hospital, I was homeschooled by my mother, who worked closely with my ever-attentive teacher; lesson plans and books were brought into the house, and I progressed steadily with the rest of my class. But in another way, I was years ahead of my peers: I was developing a taste for barley and hops. In addition to multiple medications, I was prescribed a tonic of Guinness stout and milk, thought to have beneficial properties for bacterial balance in the digestive tract. I hated the taste but liked the feel and was forced to drink the stuff daily. At the ripe age of eleven, this was my first introduction to alcohol, issued by the resident nurse, my mother. Neither of us could have possibly known then that what started off bitter would become addictively sweet to me years later.

During my recuperation, my father quit drinking, having heard the doctor's warning loud and clear that chaos and anxiety could cause me to relapse. While he'd gone dry, it would be inaccurate to say my father was in recovery. He did not have the benefits of therapy or Alcoholics Anonymous

(A.A.), which was in its infancy in Ireland at that time. He did not have the opportunity or wherewithal to explore his personal history, understand his anger, frustration, fear, and shame, or find a healthier outlet for himself and his family. My father no longer drank, an admirable achievement, but he could still be unpredictable and volatile.

My father became more religious after my illness, and we prayed the rosary daily, not just during the compulsory month of May, which was a standard requirement for Irish Catholics. A new calmness descended on our home, and our family life began to smooth out. My older three siblings had left home, so we were no longer as cramped as we had been. While I missed my brother and sisters, I was also grateful they had moved out, which meant more space in our modest house for me. That new space was filled with fresh experiences. Storytelling became a central theme in our evenings around the turf fire while the room filled with the pungent smell of burning peat, dried to be used as fuel to heat our home. My father was an enthralling narrator. He loved telling stories about his time in England, even though his disdain for the English was obvious.

Family lore has it that my father and his brothers, albeit young boys at the time, were Irish Republican Army (IRA) informers during "Cogadh na Saoirse," the Irish War of Independence, also known as the Anglo-Irish War, which was a guerrilla war fought between 1919 and 1921. Whether my father was an IRA informer or not is still under debate, but his support and devotion to the cause lasted his lifetime and made for terrific family myth-making in my youth. During the 1970s, when I was living in New York City and my other siblings were widely scattered across the globe, my parents graciously housed an IRA member recently released from prison. They kept the fact that they were housing this prisoner a secret from us, but he slept in my old childhood bed and enjoyed the luxuries of all the home improvements my earnings in New York financed. Housing a prisoner was a generous and courageous act that made me proud of my parents, while it potentially placed them both in harm's way. I suspect my parents passed off their houseguest as a distant relative or yet another of their offspring. No one in town was ever the wiser for it.

As a preadolescent, I still suffered from the shyness I'd felt as a five-year-old. Coupled with illness and the experiences I'd had in the hospital, I took comfort, refuge really, in the religion I was raised in. And with the changes my illness had brought about in my father, we developed a new bond within our Catholicism. I was dedicated to the teachings of the church, and as my beautiful gypsy friend began to fade into memory, I again imagined dedicating not just my mind and spirit to the church but my body and soul as well. After three months in the adult ward, I no longer feared death; I understood it was a part of life, of everyone's life. I thought if I could provide solace and a sense of safe shelter to others, that would be a good life, a life of meaning and purpose. What better way to accomplish that than by becoming a nun in the Catholic Church?

While I had decided to enter the convent, I had not yet shared this ambition with either parent when my mother, unwittingly, supercharged that dream for me. One day while we were in town shopping at the local market with one of my older sisters, we stopped to talk with the shop-keeper. Looking at both of us children but seeing only one, the woman remarked on my sister's beauty. Now, this is never, regardless of time, place or standing, a good thing for a younger sister to hear. Comparing the physical attributes of a gangly, awkward caterpillar with her fully formed, graceful, and gorgeously colored butterfly of an older sister is just heartless. When the shopkeeper finally looked at me, she asked, "Molly, is this also your daughter?" To which my mother replied while placing a consoling hand on my shoulder, "Yes. But this one will have to rely on her brains." My mother was totally unaware that her words pierced my heart and added to my already low self-esteem. At that moment, going into the convent felt less like a genuine and thoughtful choice to be of service to others than the obvious answer to a dilemma I didn't know I had: how was I going to be accepted by the world at large when I was seen only as a sickly, sallow-skinned, introverted waif half-hidden behind her mother's skirt and in the definite shadow of a beautiful older sister? My mother did not intend to hurt me, but in that instant, her comment revealed her personal values and the importance she placed on temporal beauty, a beauty I did not possess at age eleven.

Her reply firmly placed my two feet on a path to develop my intellect. I was an avid reader and read every novel I could get my hands on, a challenge in a town without a library. I was a strong student and enjoyed school, but I suddenly saw those traits as survival skills instead of inherent strengths. My intention had been to enter the convent at sixteen, and I knew I would not be beautiful by my mother and a shopkeeper's standards by then. My fate felt preordained.

When I finally discussed my intentions with my parents, both were encouraging. My father had a favorite expression he repeated frequently: "It might be so," and he'd say this whenever I discussed my future with him. This saying always made me feel as if I had his attention and support but with an exit ramp, knowing I wouldn't disappoint him if I changed my mind. As my adolescent years approached, I intensified my commitment to the church and attended mass regularly, not just on the obligatory Sundays.

Simultaneously, a conflict was emerging. I was growing up and out, and those adolescent hormones were reshaping me like clay in a skilled sculptor's hands. Teenage boys noticed and began asking me out. My commitment to the church wavered again as those hormones kicked in and memories of the forbidden stories told by the gypsy woman resurfaced. I was confused but happy and not just a little excited by what might unfold, depending on what path I chose to walk.

I have never been sure whether I chose the path or it chose me. But over the next couple of years, I entered a world a universe away from the convent doors. I met my first love and fell hard. Patrick was a local student at the university in Dublin. I thought he was sophisticated and worldly, and he gave me a sense of validation I'd not felt from my mother. He helped level the playing field between my beautiful older sister and me, at least in my eyes, which, I was rapidly learning, were the only eyes that counted. I was crazy about him and crazy about the way he made me feel.

My trajectory has never been the shortest distance between two points. Conflicting desires, needs, and a personal struggle with certain social conventions created dissonance within me. A cognitive, psychological, and spiritual discord began to take root in those years, a cleaving of the soul. While part of me still wanted to be a nun, I loved my boyfriend and loved being in love. I wanted to explore distant places and experience more than where I'd come from and what was tediously familiar. Not only did I want out of the poverty, violence, and dysfunction of my family life in Killorglin, I wanted to feel safe, respected for who I was, and beautiful by my own standards. My mother's comment to that shopkeeper inspired me in ways she never knew. Only many years later would I realize that folded within the bleak box of my childhood experiences lay the raw materials that would burnish me into the accomplished woman I would become. I was too young to know then, but my future would hold advanced degrees, a varied and successful career, worldly travel, love, and a relentless drive to help others. All of it sprang from those dark, lean times, those hurtful words of my mother, my father's abuse, and the terrors of my childhood.

Today we know that being a witness to trauma or being personally victimized can be severely damaging to an individual's developmental stages and the forming of successful relationships, especially intimate ones. Children who grow up in dysfunctional, abusive homes and experience emotional, physical, and/or sexual abuse are also prone to Post-Traumatic Stress Disorder (PTSD). PTSD is a mental health condition triggered by a terrifying event either personally experienced or witnessed. Symptoms may include flashbacks, nightmares, severe anxiety, and uncontrollable thoughts about the event. Left untreated, PTSD can steal a person's life away. It took me many years, many mistakes, and becoming an alcoholic just like my father before I was able to recognize symptoms of PTSD in myself. Learning something is one step, but really understanding it, living it, feeling it in your very bones, is altogether something else. Without that deep understanding, we repeat past behaviors and damage ourselves and those we love even when we know how much pain those behaviors generate. The traumas of the past are destined to be repeated in the future if they go untreated, unlearned, and unreconciled. That which is not transformed is transmitted. But I didn't know that until later. Much later.

When I was twenty-eight and living it up as a single, fun-loving flight attendant in New York City, I was thoroughly enjoying the glamorous and shallow lifestyle of attending parties, going "clubbing," and having numerous boyfriends. But all that came crashing down when, in January of 1975, I received a call informing me that my mother had suddenly died of a brain tumor at the age of sixty. Just one year later, we buried my father, who died of a heart attack at sixty-eight. Thankfully, my siblings and I had all developed more stable relationships with our parents prior to their deaths, albeit superficial on many fronts: none of us ever did talk to either of them about our childhoods or about what we'd suffered at the hands of our father. Life had not been easy for any of us adult children; we all struggled with various forms of anxiety, stress-related issues, relationship problems, alcoholism, depression, low self-esteem, and PTSD. By the time my parents died, most of us somehow had landed on the firmer ground of being survivors, not the shifting sands of victimhood. But not without a lot of difficult personal work, and certainly not always in a straight line.

I had grown particularly close with my mother once I had left home and visited her frequently. Her death was a crushing blow and, I worried, threatened to unspool the progress I was making in putting my own adult life in order. As the years passed, I also developed a loving relationship with my father, as I came to understand his demons and saw their progeny in myself. The poet Rilke captured my father's complexity perfectly when he wrote:

> *If my devils are to leave me*
> *I'm afraid my angels will take flight as well.* [2]

My parents are buried in Dromavally Burial Ground in Killorglin; all my siblings attended both funerals. On my return flight to New York after my mother's funeral, the tears were rolling down my cheeks as the Pan American 707 was rolling down the runway for takeoff. As chance would have it, I was seated next to a very compassionate nun; when she expressed her concern, I shared that my mother had just died. She was very comforting and such a deeply familiar figure to me, and for a moment it felt as if I was sitting next to an alternative version of myself, the me I had once wanted to be.

My heartbreak over my mother's death was compounded by worry about my father and wondering how he would cope without her now that he was all alone in the house. The neighbors, who long ago used to be his drinking buddies, all watched out for him and helped in many ways. My brother brought him to England to spend time with his family, and I brought him to the States later that autumn. Before he died in the spring of the following year, we made it possible for him to travel to Canada and Germany to visit his children and grandchildren, all scattered around the world by then.

The loss of both parents within such a short period of time left me reeling. I had trouble getting my bearings, so I looked for comfort in a lot of the wrong places. With both parents now gone, I had no reason to go back to Ireland. I cut myself off from where I'd come from, and I stayed gone for a long, long time. I believe my parents are the last of the family tree that will be buried in Killorglin. Their children will likely either be buried or cremated in the foreign lands we've made our adult homes in. Sorrow visits when I think of this. Some of my siblings swore they would never leave Ireland, but we all have. We say we love the green fields and the Irish Sea, and yet there's a reason, there are many painful reasons, that none of us are there.

I grew up in the shadow of the mountains and on the shores of a river. In time I would come to see those mountains as I saw my father: unmovable, formidable, and as volatile as the weather at the summit. And I saw my mother in that river. She was life-giving and course-changing by her very nature, and she carried the tears generated by my father's demons much like the river carries the mountain streams out to the sea.

Chapter II: Party in the Sky

In this modern world, air travel represents the height of luxury, and Pan Am is the biggest name in the business. The planes are glamorous, the pilots are rock stars, and the stewardesses are the most desirable women in the world . . .

—BBC Documentary, *Come Fly With Me: The Story of Pan Am*

When I was seven, as the family story goes, I informed my father I was going to travel all over the world when I grew up. I would look up at the contrails from the planes flying in and out of Shannon Airport ninety miles away and wish the in-flight crew could see me, so they would swoop down and pick me up. My imagination and desires were far-fetched and outsized in the 1950s: I had no idea what it meant to travel. But ever supportive, my father would say, "It might be so," and so I dreamt. Having been raised in the shadows of Mount Brandon, where four airplanes had gone down in the early 1940s, I was unaware of what power that mountain held for me and how, like a 3,100-foot weathervane, it pointed me in the direction of my up-in-the-air future.

After leaving high school, I worked at the local hotels in Killarney, a short distance from my hometown, serving tourists from all over the world. My curiosity was finely tuned, and I wanted to know where these visitors came from and where they were going. I admired the women's beautiful clothes and sophisticated airs. I was selected by the hotel manager to participate in management training, and part of that training took place in

Switzerland, my first plane trip. While there, I studied German and seemed to have an aptitude for languages; it did not take me long to become conversant. Soon after the training, I moved on to a position at The May Fair Hotel in London. The May Fair, dating back to 1927, was a legendary crown jewel among mansions that had been converted into hotels in the UK and today still enjoys its reputation for spectacular luxury, lavish debauchery, and unwavering discretion. My position as a management trainee had been difficult to come by, and I was thrilled, if not astounded, that I'd been hired on. My time there wound up to be brief, only about six months, though those six months proved to be fortuitous in determining my next step. That was because airline crew members frequented The May Fair, and my attention quickly gravitated away from the well-heeled tourists to watching the crew. The stunning flight attendants ("stewardesses" in those days) so impressed me as smart, classy, and elegant in their form-fitting uniforms. The pilots were handsome and suave. I was twenty-one years old, and being rather impetuous, I suddenly knew that that's what I wanted to do; that was the life I wanted to have; those women were the woman I wanted to be.

I just had no idea how to go about getting there. In questioning the flight attendants who came through The May Fair, I'd come to understand it was very difficult to join their ranks, especially if one wasn't bilingual. While I was conversant in German, I doubted I could pass myself off as truly fluent. But one day, I saw an advertisement from a small charter airline called Monarch; they were looking for German-speaking flight attendants. As I read on, I felt as if that ad had been written just for me. I applied, met all the requirements, especially the language proficiencies, and was hired in 1968 to fly charters all over the world. At Monarch, I'd acted on the declaration my seven-year-old self had made by leaving home and traveling extensively. The irony was not lost on me that the carrier of my long-held dream's fulfillment was named after the gorgeous butterfly, the one I thought I'd never become. Another common name for the monarch butterfly is a wanderer. And so, as my father used to say, "It might be so," only this time, it was meant to be.

A year later, I applied to Pan American World Airways, better known as Pan Am. Representatives of the airline were interviewing candidates in London, and when I walked into the hotel where the interviews were being held, it was like walking into a movie casting call. My heart sank; whatever bit of self-esteem I had mustered evaporated in the face of all those beautiful women gathered from all over Europe. Multiple languages were being spoken by the most elegant of creatures, and then there was me. But being Irish wound up to be an advantage when I applied; the Irish were well-liked in the US, perhaps in part because of America's love affair with the Kennedy family, which worked in my favor. That, my adeptness in German and my inherent brogue, plus my experience in hospitality—especially at The May Fair, so well known it gave me bragging rights—and having worked for Monarch all blended somehow, and I was hired on. My childhood dream of getting away from my family, out of Killorglin, and traveling around the world all came true with just one wave of the magic wand the rest of the world referred to as Pan Am. To me, my new life was nothing short of exceptional.

The story of Pan Am, what it was, what it became, and the cultural influence it would come to have, was extraordinary. Starting off in 1927 as a seaplane mail carrier service between Key West, Florida, and Havana, Cuba, it soon expanded under the visionary leadership of its founder, Juan Trippe. He opened his Cuba-bound aircraft's doors to party-seeking passengers left parched by Prohibition, flying them to the small island 105 miles off Florida's southernmost key. Trippe had a keen sense of what people wanted and what needs weren't being fulfilled, and he never hesitated to seize the advantage when he saw opportunities others didn't. He was a man ahead of his times, a "futurist." Consulting with Charles Lindbergh, the most famous pilot in the world at that time, Trippe secured access to new ports in exotic locations, using seaplanes to land in places that didn't have airports.

Originally, Pan Am hired only male flight attendants. The job of the "steward" was to row the passengers out to the seaplanes and help load them and their baggage on board. When women were hired, we were therefore called "stewardesses." By the time I joined the ranks, the cabin crew was mostly female, with a few male flight attendants who were in senior roles as pursers (chief flight attendants) and in-flight directors. And, of course, the cockpit was 100 percent male-dominated.

By the late 1930s, Pan Am's "Clippers," named in honor of the fast-moving ships of the 19th century, became the first to cross the Pacific Ocean. A decade later, the "Yankee Clipper" traveled from New York to Europe across the Atlantic. After WWII, Trippe was quoted as saying, "A tourist plane filled with enthusiastic tourists going around the world would have much more effect on destiny than the atom bomb." Never a modest man or one given to understatement, I wonder if even he had any idea what Pan Am would look like in another twenty-five years.

Under Trippe, Pan Am was the innovator of many airline standards you've likely spent your entire life taking for granted every time you board a plane, such as a pressurized cabin, the use of jumbo jets, computerized reservation systems, automated pilot programs, and in-flight messaging systems via satellite. Trippe's vision was to match the quality of his fleet with "crème de la crème" service on board and eventually to make air travel available to everyone. In 1949, his passengers were treated to champagne, large tins of beluga caviar, steak, and ice cream, and the fleet was provisioned with sleeping quarters. A decade later, on-board dining, accurately referred to as "cuisine," was out of this world, an unfathomable concept today when coach class is lucky to be given pretzels the size of quarters in a package just slightly larger than a business card. Catered by the famous French restaurant, "Maxim's de Paris," beautiful-looking, delicious meals were served by likewise beautiful-looking, delicious young women, a very intentional marketing ploy by Mr. Trippe.

Pan Am became synonymous with glamour and sophistication. While not the first airline to use jets (that distinction belonged to the British), Pan Am's innovative partnership with The Boeing Company ushered in the "jet set" with the introduction of the Boeing 707 in 1961. It allowed for transatlantic flights, the first being from New York to Paris, while cutting travel time in half. Pan Am made mass tourism a reality with expanded routes, and owned Intercontinental Hotels and Resorts, still in operation today under the name of IHG, with 5,300 hotels across one-hundred countries. Developed with the same eye toward luxury and the same savvy in branding, the hotel subsidiary was originally started by Trippe after a breakfast meeting at the White House with President Franklin D. Roosevelt in 1946, where the two men put their heads together to help Latin America's need for development resources. The first hotel, The Grande Hotel in Belem, Brazil, opened later that same year, with expansion throughout Latin America and the Caribbean shortly following before developing property in the Middle East, Eastern Europe, and the U.S. The hotels also served to house the airline's crews and passengers in locations where accommodations that matched the luxury of the airline were not otherwise available.

By the early 1960s, the airline's blue globe logo (referred to in the press as the "blue meatball") was second only to Coca-Cola in terms of public recognition, but its product placement and merchandising campaigns were second to none. Brilliant marketing, not to mention political alliances that resulted in exclusive international routes, made Pan Am the premier airline of the late 60s and '70s. It was "the" place to be and to be seen, and anyone who was anyone was frequently listed on the passenger manifest. Pan Am flight #101, from Heathrow to New York City, brought the Beatles to America for their first visit on February 7, 1964; the company logo was prominently displayed directly behind their mop-haired heads during their first U.S. press conference. Elizabeth Taylor and Richard Burton, Ava Gardner, Ingrid Bergman, Marilyn Monroe, and Joe DiMaggio (that other Yankee Clipper), Paul Newman, Sean Connery, Barbra Streisand, and The Rat Pack—these are just some of the names and faces, rich, famous, and infamous alike, flying Pan Am. Even if you weren't on board but instead watching television in your living room or taking in a movie that would have set you back all the 93 cents to attend, you could, by proxy, have the Pan Am experience. *I love Lucy*, *The Beverly Hillbillies*, and *The Saint* all featured scenes of, or on, Pan Am flights in the 1950s and '60s. Dozens of movies dating back as early as 1933 (*Flying Down to Rio* with Fred Astaire and Ginger Rogers on a Pan Am Clipper "flying boat"), the first two James Bond films, *Dr. No* and *From Russia With Love*, 1968's seminal Stanley Kubrick epic, *2001: A Space Odyssey*, all featured Pan Am planes. Cultural icons such as Humphrey Bogart, Rosalind Russell, Steve McQueen, Clint Eastwood, and Susan Sarandon have been seen on board Pan Am flights on the silver screen throughout the years in between.

But perhaps the most popular film featuring Pan Am was 2002's Oscar-nominated *Catch Me If You Can*, starring Leonardo DiCaprio and Tom Hanks. Based on the true yet unbelievable story of Frank W. Abagnale, the colorful imposter and check-forger, DiCaprio plays the charismatic trickster who, at age sixteen, impersonated a Pan Am pilot because he wanted to fly around the globe without paying for it. And because, of course, he was subject to the ultimate male fantasy of those times: being swarmed by a bevy of Pan Am stewardesses. Calling the airline to report his pilot's uniform—he didn't own one—had been lost after sending it to the hotel's laundry service—he wasn't a hotel guest—he obtained a regulation Pan Am uniform along with a fake airline employee ID. Already a skilled forger, he then produced a Federal Aviation Administration (FAA) pilot's license.

Over the next twenty-four months, Abagnale flew more than a million miles on more than 250 flights to twenty-six countries, all by "deadheading," a practice all the airlines used by which they provided passenger seats to their crews to get them to destinations where their scheduled routes departed. As a (pretend) company pilot, Abagnale was also able to stay at hotels for free and get his meals for free, all of which were billed back to Pan Am, who unblinkingly paid for the sixteen-year-old kid's really good time. It took a lot of chutzpah and smarts to bilk the largest and most profitable airline in the world. He did so successfully by never flying on an actual Pan Am flight—although Pan Am 707s and 747s are featured in the movie— because he thought he'd be caught. He also never actually flew a plane but was invited by pilots in the cockpit on more than one occasion to take the controls, which he was able to do by enabling autopilot. He states in his book that he was "very much aware that I had been handed custody of 140 lives, my own included . . . because I couldn't fly a kite."[3]

Knowing the crew—especially women—was the public face of the company, Pan Am executives employed stringent requirements as to who should represent them. By 1960, young women were lining up to get on board. Pan Am was *the* glamorous career destination for young women from all over the world for nearly half of the twentieth century.

It was this airline, this cultural phenomenon, that this girl went to work for. Pan Am dispatched a recruiting team to Europe, where they scouted for "the look": women were very carefully chosen for their height (not shorter than 5'2" and not taller than 5'9"), figures (well-proportioned yet slim, and not over 140 pounds regardless of height), faces (symmetrical and a smile of all teeth with absolutely no visible gum line)[4], and their sophistication, meaning they appeared calm, cool, and supremely self-assured. Most were well-educated and multilingual. By these standards, I met the criteria.

But my vision of myself in those days wasn't defined by any of those descriptors. I saw myself still as the awkward, bookish type as if my self-perception had frozen at age fourteen. And yet I had to allow . . . maybe I was wrong? The recruiters had chosen me, ME, at a time when fewer than 3 percent of applicants were accepted. One pilot said of his female colleagues, "They had curves as nice as the airplane's." Another was less metaphorical and more pragmatic: "I picked out one to marry on every single flight . . . they were gorgeous women."[5] But Pan Am went beyond this, and by today's standards, their hiring practices would generate reams of discrimination lawsuits. Part of the interview process was a catwalk, where we were told to walk forward, stand, pivot slowly 360 degrees, then turn and walk away: we were being inspected and judged like cattle at an auction. If hired, we were given very little time to fold up our current lives, regardless of where we lived, and report to New York City and then onto Miami for intensive six-week training. Job orientation was in-depth and far-reaching and even included training on how to deliver a baby, should that blessed event unexpectedly commence at 30,000 feet.

To be honest, it's still incredulous to me that this shy, small village girl became a face representing Pan Am. My face, in fact, literally became the face of Pan Am a few years later when I was photographed by the famous American fashion photographer, Francesco Scavullo (1921–2004), who had developed the concept of the magazine "cover girl," celebrating female beauty, sexuality, and glamour. More than three decades of his fifty-year career were spent shooting covers for *Cosmopolitan*. Pan Am used the photos he took of me for their public relations and marketing campaigns in Eastern Europe and Central America.

Hired at the height of these heady times in 1970, I was relocated from London, and after completing my initial training in Miami, I was moved to New York City, where Pan Am's flagship terminal, called "Worldport," was in the John F. Kennedy (JFK) International Airport. We were unchaperoned and set loose in the city, which was a dangerous place in those years, to find our own housing and find our own way. I found a place close to Harlem with three other flight attendants; we lived there for about a year. We had no money, we had no common sense, and we had an abundance of no situational awareness. At the time, I was not aware of the high crime rate in our neighborhood; I'd just arrived from London, and I was naïve. One morning around six, standing in my Pan Am uniform alone at the bus stop for the ride to JFK, a car pulled up and the driver, sticking his head out the window, offered to take me there. I momentarily considered it; it was tempting. As I said, I was naïve. My whole body suddenly reacted in animal fear; I sensed his intentions, which weren't good. Fortunately, other people were arriving at the bus stop, and they immediately engaged me in conversation, perhaps sensing something themselves. The driver floored the accelerator pedal and was gone. You would have thought this brush with near danger would have been instructive, that I'd become more aware and see I was potential prey. But no. My roommates and I continued to run heedless and reckless around the city, out at all hours of the day and night, half drunk and falling off our barstools with just one look from a handsome face. I was nearly assaulted by a roommate's boyfriend late one night before being able to shove him off. I think it was nothing short of divine intervention that saved us all. That, and the fact that none of us were grounded for long. I was assigned to fly international flights exclusively, from New York to Africa, Asia, Europe, South America, and the Middle East. I was flying three weeks every month, and I had never been happier.

Like the stewardesses, the Pan Am pilots were just as glamorous and just as well-trained. Many had been in the service and brought with them a formidable presence, exuding confidence and competence with each swaggered step. They also brought mechanical and electrical acumen; they were prepared to take care of any malfunction on board, including changing an engine. But unlike the stewardesses, some of the pilots were known to be crass and unsophisticated, and some treated us poorly or made outlandish demands. Exceptions existed, of course, like Captain Charlie Blair, who was as handsome and debonair as Cary Grant in *An Affair to Remember*. He dated and later married famous passenger Maureen O'Hara, who was not only known as Ireland's first great Hollywood star but also as the

"Queen of Technicolor." On a flight from New York to Shannon, Ireland, they were my first-class passengers, and they extended a personal invitation to join them at their home in Glengariff, County Cork. I still kick myself for not accepting that invitation to spend an evening with the rich and famous. Aristotle Onassis was one of my first-class passengers on a flight from Paris to New York once. At the time, he owned Olympic Airlines, then based out of Athens, so it was surprising that he'd be flying a competitor. He was married to Jacqueline Kennedy at the time, which was regrettable because despite being in my early 20s and he old enough to be my grandfather, I would have married him on the spot. He was that charming. At the time, I was dating several prominent passengers, including Lars Schmidt, the Swedish millionaire, successful film and theater producer/ director who had been married to one of the world's most beautiful actresses, Ingrid Bergman. We had been introduced at a party in New York by the Swedish hostess and began a brief, though meaningful relationship. He had friends all over the world and in royal places; we spent a week alone at HRH Princess Margaret's Caribbean villa Les Jolies Eaux on the island of Mustique. After that affair, the acclaimed news anchor Peter Jennings, a frequent passenger, wrote me a personal letter on airline letterhead asking me out. I've kept that letter all these years and frequently wondered why I demurred. Many of the stewardesses were known to have a "steady boyfriend" at their home base, and this was true for me as well. But we were fond of saying, "When the wheels are up, anything goes." Of course, not everyone was fooling around and being irresponsible. But I sure was. I sought out the partiers among my peers and my passengers both at home and on the job. Partying was my second full-time vocation.

As if all that wasn't keeping me busy enough, I was also dating quite a few pilots at the time, most of whom were fine, upstanding men. I never really gave any of them a chance, though, thinking they were players and womanizers when, in fact, it was me who filled those dancing shoes. It was around that time when I met one of the great loves of my life. Ahmed (not his real name) was an ambassador from the Middle East to the United Nations. We didn't meet on board; a mutual friend in New York introduced me to him. I'm not sure if it was love at first sight, but we both certainly fell deeply in love quickly and proceeded to have a long, involved relationship that spanned many years. Since he was an ambassador, he was obliged to host many dignitaries and throw frequent dinner parties at his home. My Pan Am training came in very handy as I played the role of his partner, the gracious hostess, entertaining diplomats from around the world. We loved traveling together; our trips took us to Bermuda, Mexico, Paris, and many other locations. I saw everything through different eyes when I was on his arm; the world looked more beautiful, more exotic, and exciting when we were together.

One of my most memorable trips with Ahmed was to a casino in London, where a friend of his, a gambler, gave me the equivalent of $5000 in casino chips to gamble. I promptly cashed them in, preferring instead to go on a shopping spree at Harrods. I wanted gifts to take to my sister the next day. She was living in Dagenham, a marginal neighborhood in Essex; the disparity between her lifestyle and mine couldn't have been starker. I arrived in my ambassador boyfriend's chauffeur-driven Rolls Royce bearing gifts from the department store when shopping at Harrods was well beyond her reach, her needs, and her wildest dreams. I was embarrassed by my well-intended but lavish display.

My father had come to New York after about a year into my romance with the ambassador. Ahmed picked us up in his chauffeured car and took us to one of the city's finest restaurants. Later that night, as my dad and I discussed the evening and my love for this man, he responded with, "He's a fine man, Joanie (his nickname for me). It's just a shame that he's already married." I would have been less surprised if he'd just told me I'd been conceived by leprechauns and sold to my family at birth for a Guinness pint. Rightly, my father pointed out that a man of the ambassador's stature from a middle-eastern country would most certainly have a wife as a necessary social norm, if not a mandatory social accessory. I had been too much in love to see it. For all my newfound sophistication and exposure to worldly ways, it was my simple, uneducated but wise and perceptive father who pointed out how far my moral compass had leaned away from true north. Despite Ahmed telling me he'd leave his wife for this great love we shared, which also would have meant he'd have to leave his post and his career all in one fell swoop, I sensed that this would be tantamount to a priest leaving the church. It took me another three years, but I eventually broke it off.

In a very real sense, Pan Am stewardesses were treated as brand products: uniformity of design, color, size, and shape was mandatory. While my employment there came at the tail end of the most rigid requirements, I was still subject to many. We were all given Dale Carnegie's seminal book, *How to Win Friends and Influence People*; we were all given the same make-up kits, containing the exact same products in the exact same shades. Deviation was disallowed: we couldn't have highlights or any type of artificial color in our hair, and if any of us couldn't wear the Pan Am authorized Revlon "Persian Melon" lipstick and matching nail polish, we had to receive written permission from the "grooming supervisor." Eagle eyes were a requirement of that job. You could count on her to find it all: a wayward strand of hair, chipped nail polish, a loose hemline. If you had a visible bruise, you could be pulled from working your shift; if you'd been sunbathing and reported to work with a fresh bloom of freckles or tanned, you could be suspended. We were subjected to frequent weight checks. The humiliating little practice known as the "girdle check," which involved wearing a girdle to ensure all the stewardesses looked sleek, was blessedly tabled by the time I came along.

The Pan Am stewardess uniforms, immediately identifiable in that decade by the pillbox hat, wrist-level white gloves, and jackets with little buttons, were the brainchild of top Hollywood costume designers such as Edith Head, who won an astounding eight Academy Awards for Best Costume Design while being nominated for twenty-seven others. Our look was all clean, crisp lines; attractive, smart, and self-consciously un-sexy. This, too, was branding. A certain aloofness was intentionally cultivated; we were to be seen as beautiful but not bed-able, in contrast to how National Airlines portrayed their stewardesses in ad campaigns such as "Fly Me" and Continental's overtly suggestive slogan "We really move our tail for you." We were to look like women men would take home to meet their mothers, not those they'd leave money on the dresser for "afterward."

That being said, there was a whole lot of hanky-panky going on. This was the early 1970s, the era of sex, drugs, and rock and roll. The pill had received FDA approval as a contraceptive; free love was not only sanctioned but encouraged. Married men would slip their wedding rings into their pants pocket as they boarded the plane, using "Man Tan" to tint the suspect white band of skin to a more sun-kissed tone. These chronically randy male passengers seemed to believe that Pan Am had pre-qualified us as their future wives, or at least wife-for-a-night, as a personal service bundled into the price of the ticket. And to be fair, they weren't the only ones looking to add a little pep in their step. We were young, free, and single; we were on a pedestal that men idealized and other women dreamed of reaching. What was good for the gander was equally good for the goose.

Juan Trippe had been working closely with Boeing to create a new craft capable of carrying more people at lower fares over longer distances. After first saying it was "impossible," Boeing's Chairman, Bill Allen, told Trippe, "If you'll buy it, I'll build it," to which Trippe replied, "If you'll build it, I'll buy it." The two men shook hands, and so began the gestational period of bringing forth another bellwether aeronautic design that would forever change travel while simultaneously shrinking the globe, making pretty much anywhere and everywhere attainable for pretty much everyone.[6]

The new Boeing 747 jumbo jet's debut flight was in January of 1970. It was a behemoth, more than twice the size of its predecessor, the 707, carrying more than four hundred passengers spread across two aisles and weighing 750,000 pounds. It was issued in the new "wide-body" class of passenger planes, which was not at all what Trippe had visualized. His dream was a double-decker design, which the lead engineer on the 747 labeled "a turkey." It took a Boeing executive's visit to the Pan Am boardroom, which, serendipitously, measured the same width and height as the proposed wide-body, to get Trippe to relinquish his double-decker vision. Taking in the dimensions of his boardroom as if seeing it for the very first time, he was impressed and conceded. As with the previous Pan Am fleets, this new class brought innovations that would become standard throughout the industry, such as the cabin being organized into "rooms" divided by galleys and lavatories, vertical sidewalls resulting in higher ceilings, and the first "high-bypass" turbofan engine, making it quieter, more powerful, and improving fuel efficiency, which in turn meant flying further, faster.

Pan Am launched an ambitious promotional campaign across the globe, inviting the public onto the tarmac and then up the stairs into the 747, whose shadow eclipsed the 707s and Douglas DC-8s parked next to it in an impressive display of scale juxtaposition, like that of Jonah and the whale. In fact, the pilots christened the 747 "The Whale." In its first year, the 747 flew 11 million passengers across 20 billion miles; the public had gone wild. The crew, well, not so much. One pilot compared the 747 to flying a building. Depth perception took some real getting used to, as did the small galleys that were used to prepare meals for more than four hundred hungry travelers. We used words like "chaotic" and "nightmare" to describe working on the new planes.[6] It would take another two and a half decades to learn exactly how nightmarish the design of the 747 truly was.

Despite the excitement of going to foreign ports on several continents and being enthralled with the glitz of London, Tokyo, Paris, Rio, Rome, Cairo, Tehran, and all the other fabulous cities that were part of my regular route and regardless of my home base being in the "city that never sleeps," New York . . . and notwithstanding the fact that my childhood wish was to have *exactly* the life I now had . . . I was homesick. Even though this was everything I'd ever wanted, even though I was figuratively and literally on top of the world, even though this, and even though that, I felt a yawning emptiness. I may have been lovely on the outside, but on the inside, there was ripping at the seams. While I was an eager participant in that crazy lifestyle while living in NYC and staying at luxurious ports of call, I was uncomfortable; I was not at peace. I hated leaving my ambassador boyfriend, so I made numerous "bids" (requests) to have overnight layovers so I could get back to New York as quickly as possible, but of course, he wasn't always around. Despite his presence and that of other lovers in my life, drinking had become my true romance and constant companion. My fellow flight attendants seemed to be enjoying themselves, and from the outside, it looked like I was, too. It seemed that alcohol was the elixir that gave me confidence and the feeling of sophistication; it was an impressive mask to hide my low self-esteem. Alcohol also skewed my moral compass, and I behaved badly, according to my sober moral compass, when I was under the influence. Of course, while nursing the inevitable hangover and feeling demoralized and ashamed the next morning, I'd drink again that night to escape those feelings. And because I liked the smell and taste of it, I liked how it made me feel by dulling my feelings altogether. This vicious cycle continued for seven years during my flying career. I wasn't aware that a gap, like a sinkhole, was lurking just under the surface, and its boundaries were creeping ever wider. A deep disturbance was rippling through me, which threatened to swallow me whole. I had no idea I had a drinking problem.

And so, I did what many young adults in their 20s do: I masked my fear and discomfort within my own skin by putting on my game face, highest heels, and shortest dress. I let my hair down, and I tossed all caution, not to mention discernment, to the proverbial winds. I partied as if the end of days was a factual certainty and was due to arrive a week from Thursday. I wanted to lose that lonely, sad girl staring back at me from under the surface of the polished Pan Am flight attendant in the mirror. I wanted to eviscerate the childhood that was so firmly rooted within me. I wanted to bring forth a warrior, an indestructible, invulnerable Woman. I thought if I acted as one, I'd become one. And so, I looked for her in the bottom of liquor bottles, on the arms of men, and between the sheets. Any hopes I'd had of becoming a nun were now pooled around my ankles and tangled up with my finest French lingerie.

Other than the sluggish body and foggy head of the hangover, I had not realized any negative consequences of my drinking. Everyone was doing it. We were young, pretty, and resourceful, and I knew how to "cover my ass" at work. I would compensate for the reckless nights by being overly accommodating and working the least desirable cabin position during the day, which usually meant working the first-class galley.

One morning while leaving Rome en route to Beirut and Tehran, I had a crippling hangover. The first officer and I had been up together all night, and we were both addle-brained. As I began serving pre-takeoff drinks, I noticed how friendly and solicitous the couple seated in 1 A and B were acting. They asked how I was doing. I told them I had a terrible flu and couldn't wait to get to Tehran to crawl into bed. The gentleman, looking a bit too pleased, said, "What you need is a beer! You have a hangover!" I was mortified; I thought I was hiding it quite well. We landed in Beirut amid yet another political crisis; actually, we had a military escort for landing. Some of the flight attendants and passengers were distressed about the political situation there, but my most pressing concern was getting over that hangover. By the time we landed in Tehran, I was feeling better; so good, in fact, I was ready to go out on the town. I spent those next seven years bouncing from drunken, fun-loving nights to nursing hangovers the next morning so that by the time my workday ended, I was ready to do it all over again, again and again.

I began to feel a different kind of internal struggle taking place inside me. I knew in my heart that this party girl was not me. Or she was a part of me I'd grown weary of, felt embarrassed by. The fact was I didn't know who I was, but I was becoming aware that the actions and behaviors I was expressing were no longer making me feel strong, confident, and invulnerable. Something was changing; my elixir was losing its masking properties. I became increasingly distraught by what I was doing. When I partied, I could no longer talk myself out of the shame and remorse I felt the next day. I began to suffer in a new, unfamiliar way which only later could I identify as a kind of existential angst. I felt lost, and I began longing for an understanding of why I was behaving the way I was.

It would take me nearly a decade to find my way clear of all this, but finally, in 1978, I enrolled in a recovery program. It would take another dozen years before I came to understand and eventually began the difficult work of merging the duality within myself—the worldly pretender and the traumatized child—and placed myself on a road I was proud to walk.

My last drink was that night we arrived in Tehran. A girlfriend and I had gone out with the friends of the Shah. We were all throwing back drinks at a high-class discotheque called the Cheminée, where I was seated next to the Shah's brother. Three sheets to the wind, I started pontificating on the political state of the country and forecasting a civil revolution within the next five years. I punctuated my statement by declaring the Shah an unparalleled asshole, all while sitting next to his brother. Only under the clear light of the following day did I realize who the real asshole had been the night before. I was a young, out-of-control, naïve, foolish girl whose use and abuse of alcohol could have gotten her beheaded and dumped in the desert, never to be found.

We returned to the hotel for a 4:00 a.m. departure. I was still drunk; in fact, while I had worked flights hungover plenty of times in the past, this was the first time I reported drunk onto a flight. The crew and captain all covered for me; my dark glasses shielded my light-sensitive eyes. But what they couldn't cover was my own self-inflicted indignity. Our flight was bound for Rome, and when I walked into my hotel room there, I fell to my knees and cried.

My cry for help in the very city that historically had been the seat of church authority now looks to be prophetical. Seven years after I became a stewardess for Pan Am, here I was in the city that most represented a return to my moral code and to the God-based center of my own life. The lifestyle I'd embraced as a stewardess, the stuff my dreams had been built on, had become the very thing that placed me in harm's way. When I returned to New York, I began to see a psychotherapist and started the hard work of looking at myself, my family of origin, my father's rage and drinking, my mother's compliance and her hardships, my childhood traumas, and how these elements all merged to shape my behavior. I also placed myself in a 12 Step alcohol recovery program, and I became a dedicated member; I remain a dedicated member these forty years later. I embarked on a very painful, arduous journey of self-discovery and healing, which still has no end date.

It was around this time that I met my future husband, Sean. A mutual friend introduced us in the autumn of 1979 when I was thirty-two years old; he was forty-one. When I met Sean, I wasn't interested in being in another serious relationship since I'd recently broken it off with the ambassador. But he was alluring, good-looking, successful, and extremely persuasive. He'd been born in Ireland and lived in England for many years, working in finance and traveling extensively, especially to South America, as one of the commodities he traded was coffee. By the time we met, he was a successful Wall Street executive, cultured, elegant, attentive, and "a man about town," which meant he most certainly knew how to woo a woman. In today's parlance, we'd say Sean had game. He was an experienced traveler, a bonus for this globetrotter because I could never be with someone who thought I was referring to Texas when I said "Paris." Sean was not too thrilled that I was a flight attendant; he was concerned, of course, about the possibilities of my fooling around with pilots and passengers. Even though I consistently reassured him I was not interested in others, his jealousy was formidable. Despite that, our relationship continued to develop. I thought he would feel more secure with enough time; remember, in 1979, I didn't yet have a psychology degree, which would have informed me otherwise! Our relationship was exciting; we enjoyed the cultural stimulation of New York City, going to museums, Broadway shows, and fine restaurants. We married eight months after we met, in May 1980. Looking back, I can see the fault line in this impetuous decision, given I had just begun to take a hard look at who I was and why I behaved the way I did. Unraveling, sorting out, and looking closely at oneself is excruciating and can be utterly destabilizing, even as the goal is one of greater stability and health. I didn't view Sean so much as a "savior" as much as I thought the commitment and structure of marriage would help me regain a sense of emotional security when I felt so adrift. But I didn't have that insight at the time. I was simply thrilled to say yes when he asked.

We had a religious ceremony at the United Nations Chapel, and my brother, Patrick, who had flown in from England, proudly walked me down the aisle. My younger sister, Kathleen, was my bridesmaid, and my niece, Heidi, was also in attendance. We were married in the chapel because Sean was divorced, which prevented us from taking our vows in the Catholic Church. He'd had a long-term marriage of about twenty years to a German-Jewish woman whose father was a psychiatrist from Berlin, and who'd been instrumental in saving children during the Second World War by helping them relocate to England. Sean and his wife had a son and a daughter, both teenagers by the time we married. They lived in London with their mother, visiting us during vacations. I think it was their age and the many miles between us that prevented closeness from deeply taking root. The four of us never really functioned as a family unit; Sean and I were each other's immediate family, and we were occasionally visited by these lovely young adults.

One of the things that attracted us to one another, I think, was how different each of us was from anyone we'd known before. We each brought the "greener grass," the thing we longed for: I was a reprieve from his serious responsibilities as a parent and the breadwinner of his family and the stresses of his career; I was younger, adventurous, worldly, and unencumbered by anything other than my job. In return, he brought to me a sense of maturity and stability I found irresistible. He made me feel safe.

Under Christian law, marriage was considered a sacred institution, not only a legal bond but also a spiritual bond witnessed by God, which could never be broken. While I was an American citizen by then, Ireland, the country of our birth and the bedrock of our cultural roots, didn't legalize divorce until 1997. By the time we married, I was no longer a practicing Catholic, but those roots ran deep and wide. And while I no longer attended church, I had a spiritual life, believed wholeheartedly in God, and prayed daily. The idea of marrying a divorced man had never been in my view, but sometimes we give ourselves the biggest surprises in our lives. The wedding at the UN chapel was officiated by an evangelical minister, and it was a beautiful ceremony. Our guests were Wall Street financiers and flight attendants, "pretty people" representing a snapshot of the most American ideals of financial success and physical beauty. Sean and I had an elegant reception at a private country club in New Jersey, followed by a brief honeymoon in the Hamptons, with more extensive international travel later that year.

Sean's discomfort surrounding my career, which had expressed itself as jealousy while we were courting, morphed into pressure once we married. The nine-year difference between us likely contributed to his opinion that because we didn't need the money, there wasn't any reason why I should work. His was not the generation of women's liberation. But I loved my job, the travel, my friendships with colleagues, and the adventures we always seemed to get ourselves into. I didn't want to quit, but now, as a married woman, I looked for a compromise to appease Sean by taking extended unpaid leave. We took this opportunity to travel a lot; we visited Ireland, England, Italy, Brazil, and Japan. We were great traveling companions, shared a similar sense of humor, and had the time of our lives.

I soon used the extended leave to return to school and pursue my degree in psychology. Sean was very supportive financially and emotionally and encouraged me to complete my education. Those prayers I'd offered up to God in that hotel room in Rome were heard. What neither of us knew at the time was that the more immersed I became in the study of psychology and the more deeply I began to look at myself, the more fragile our relationship became. As my personal insights expanded, allowing me to question my motivations, my choices, my drinking, my various sources of shame, my relationships with family members, my cultural background— all the components that create the self—the more difficult I found it to function in the ways and in the places that came before. There's an old expression attributed to Socrates: "The unexamined life is not worth living." For me, learning how to examine my own life began to illuminate my inability to live the life I'd been living. I've come to accept my part in the breakdown of our marriage. I had placed myself on a path that was divergent from Sean's, and I was becoming a different woman than the one he'd fallen in love with. In all fairness, he had a right to be confused, disappointed, and angry. We sought counseling and tried hard to make it work. Neither of us wanted to divorce; he'd already experienced that once and despite the fun-loving lifestyle I'd embraced for years, at heart, I was still an Irish Catholic and believed in the sanctity of marriage. We spent ten years pushing against the current before mutually agreeing to divorce in 1991.

I felt like a failure, ashamed I couldn't make our marriage work. It was a very painful, confusing time for me: as much as I was learning to understand myself, I couldn't comprehend how Sean and I could fundamentally be so fond of each other, be true friends, love each other, and yet be unable to navigate marriage. He was an ethical, kind, and generous man, and I loved him deeply. That saying we've all heard about needing to love yourself before you can love someone else, I learned then, is true. I did love him, but because I did not love myself, I felt fundamentally unworthy. No matter how much he poured into me, I was a sieve; it wouldn't hold, it couldn't stick. A year after the divorce, when I visited Ireland with my American cousins, the shame I felt was still so raw that I enlisted them in a conspiracy to lie to our other family members by saying my husband was too busy at work to accompany me. I couldn't face the truth, let alone speak it.

Sean and I were able to find our way back to closeness, albeit a very different kind, and we maintained our friendship for the next eighteen years until his death in 2009. He was diagnosed with esophageal cancer and had returned to Ireland to live out his last days surrounded by his extended Irish family. I was left to grieve his death many physical and emotional miles away in California. I keep a framed photo of Sean on my bookshelf, and I never remarried. He was as close as I ever got to finding that particular kind of comfort that only life partners experience.

As I advanced through my studies in school, I developed subspecialties in chemical dependency counseling and crisis psychology. At this time, I was still flying and had no desire to work as a counselor; I merely wanted the education to better understand myself. Or at least that's what I thought. But sometimes, life has other plans for us; my "daimon"—in Greek mythology, my divine power, fate, or guardian angel—had other designs that would soon make themselves clear. But at the time, nothing was clear. I became increasingly isolated from my friends and colleagues; I had one foot in two disparate worlds. While flying, I spent my layovers studying while my closest friends were still out partying. This created disconnection and the return of loneliness. But I was fully committed, and as my mother had hoped for us when we were young, I received my degree, eventually earning a master's and then progressing to earn a PhD. While I was anything but proud of what had led me to this achievement, I knew I had fulfilled my mother's dream. Had she witnessed the commencement, decked out in my cap and gown, I knew she would have beamed with pride. Maybe for the first time in my adult life, I felt I had earned that pride.

After earning my undergraduate degree in psychology—I had studied at both the State University of New York (SUNY) and at Fordham University, also in New York—I pursued a professional program and earned certification as an alcohol recovery counselor. I then joined the Professional Standards Committee for the flight attendants union, becoming a peer counselor helping other flight attendants suffering from alcoholism and other substance abuse problems. This was my first foray into helping others as a result of first helping myself, the literal manifestation of placing the oxygen mask on oneself before placing it on another.

While I was working on ways to improve myself, Juan Trippe was successfully working on his own dreams of improvement by making air travel accessible to the masses. While the 747 ushered in affordable travel for the general population, it also announced the end of an era. The glamorous days of the jet-set were waning, and in their place, a lowest common denominator filled the seats and the galleys. Passengers no longer dressed to the nines; they now came on board in shorts, T-shirts, and flip-flops. Louis Vuitton matching luggage sets were replaced with backpacks and duffle bags. And with so many people now on board, Pan Am could no longer afford to offer fine French cuisine or large tubs of caviar. The company's business model seemed to flip as soon as the new model of plane rolled out: instead of high quality being sold to an exclusive demographic, higher volume sales at a lower price point became the new norm.

Meanwhile, the company itself had become unwieldy, with tens of thousands of employees scattered across sixty-two countries. As the calendar pages gave way to the next season, so came changes in quick succession at the company. The brand once synonymous with sophistication and luxury was becoming "The face of America," nearly an extension of the US government. The airline operated and maintained a missile range for the US Air Force, and it was rumored to be cooperating with the CIA, flying supplies and personnel into Berlin during the Cold War while the Soviets, then controlling East Germany, surrounded the city. Pan Am also had a role in the debacle that was Vietnam. The airline made more flights there than any other US carrier, hauling troops back and forth, and it evacuated children orphaned by the war in "Operation Babylift."

Juan Trippe retired as president of Pan Am in 1968. Within the next few years, the astounding trajectory of Pan Am began to feel the pull of gravity reversing its course. Between the recession in the 1970s, the spike in oil prices, over-expansion, and Trippe's absence at the helm, the airline lost altitude. The Airline Deregulation Act of 1978 brought new competition and a further decline in ticket prices. Two years later, Pan Am purchased National Airlines to expand its US market, but that came with a crippling price tag that nearly buried the company. To correct its course, it bailed out of the hotel chains and sold off the missile ranges and Pacific routes, which, in retrospect, was an early death knell. The Pacific routes had built Pan Am's legacy; selling them was an act of desperation, like the royal family selling off Buckingham Palace. United Airlines' parent company, UAL, purchased the Pacific routes for $290 million, not nearly enough to stem the hemorrhaging. And if all that combined wasn't bad enough, Pan Am suddenly became a target of international terrorist attacks and hijackings, in part because it had been the flagship US carrier for so many years. That "blue meatball" logo so proudly displayed on the tail suddenly began to look like a bullseye. All attempts at triage were failing, even while it served as an extension of US interests, one of which I was a part of.

In 1979, I was involved in a rescue operation in Tehran, Iran. We were an all-volunteer crew, including the pilots. Three Pan Am 747s evacuated eight hundred American men, women, and children in the civilian exodus out of the city when the country was besieged by violence and civil unrest. Many of the Americans had been living in Tehran as contractors for various American companies and had been trapped for days in their homes. Their lives were threatened whenever they ventured out to the grocery store or to escort their children to school. When they were finally evacuated to safety, each was allowed only one suitcase and handbag; the rest of their lives were suddenly abandoned and left behind.

There had been a caravan of twelve buses, escorted by armed guards from Ayatollah Ruhollah Khomeini's volunteer army, who brought the Americans from the embassy to the airport. The airport, not yet officially reopened for business, was guarded by roadblocks and armed militia. En route, the caravan drove past Teheran University, which had become an armed bastion of leftist protestors. There, about a hundred students milled around, some crouching behind sandbags serving as platforms for machine guns. Banners with hammer and sickle symbols and Islamic slogans flapped overhead. One student was caught on camera smiling, giving the victory sign, and yelling, "Bye-bye!" They were not saddened by our departure, and we were likewise not saddened to be leaving such a volatile situation.

The Americans had been processed for travel the night before at the embassy or at the Hilton Hotel and had their passports taken by embassy employees, a standard procedure. The passengers carried receipts certifying their place on the plane; they'd been handed boarding passes in exchange for their passports. One evacuee, exhausted and traumatized that she had to leave her Iranian husband in Tehran, became hysterical when one of Khomeini's soldiers shoved the barrel of his machine gun in her chest, demanding her travel documents. "Passport! Passport!" he screamed in her face. Escalating the exchange, she yelled back at him in defiance because, of course, she, like the rest of us, wasn't in possession of her passport. Fortunately, I was standing right next to her; I grabbed her arm firmly and reminded her that we were still on the ground in Tehran and not yet free. She calmed down, and the soldier moved on, content enough, apparently, with her boarding pass. The razor's edge between danger and safety was very thin.

There were also several hundred British and French citizens at the airport, waiting to be evacuated on Royal Air Force and Air France airliners. The British left during the day, but Air France announced at noon that its flight had been temporarily canceled, leaving passengers angry or in tears. Some had been trapped for days in their homes prior to their planned evacuation, pinned down by the fighting all around them, paralyzed by threats against their lives. The canceled flight, the canceled escape to safety, was more than they could take.

After an all-day wait on the tarmac, the first two Pan American 747s took off with 405 Americans; another 747 and a C-141 military transport were in line to take off next, carrying the balance of the evacuees. We flew out of Tehran like bats out of hell. When my plane's captain announced that we had finally cleared Iranian airspace, a joyous uproar from both passengers and crew filled the cabin. At the time of this evacuation, the crew was based in Frankfurt, Germany. When we finally landed at the air force base near Frankfurt, we were treated like celebrities by the media and passengers alike, who stood applauding this all-volunteer crew as we made our way through the terminal. Even though this was probably the most dangerous situation I had ever found myself in with Pan Am, it was far and away the most gratifying.

As part of my recovery from alcohol addiction, I hung up my couture stewardess uniforms in 1986. I transferred into Pan Am's medical department as their first corporate manager of the Employee Assistance Program (EAP). This was a highly coveted position, and the five airline employee unions were all jockeying to put forth their strongest candidates. I was not particularly interested in the position, but my flight manager recommended me and set up an interview with the medical director, Dr. John McCann. My initial interview went well. In a clear statement of magnanimity, not to mention ambivalence, I recall telling Dr. McCann I would be willing to help whoever got the job. But somehow, Dr. McCann saw through me, or saw me through my own guarded persona, and offered me the position.

My new role was very demanding. I worked long hours and commuted from my home in New Jersey to JFK. Essentially, my duties were to educate management and unions on the complexities of chemical dependency and to encourage early identification and referral into a recovery program. Working as the EAP manager for the airline was challenging; I was to be advising others on what had been, for the last decade or so, so difficult for me to do myself. When I had been working on my psychology degree, I thought I was doing so to better understand myself. And that was true. But my new role in the EAP had given way to a new understanding, another truth, and that was how rewarding it felt to be helping others.

Therapy had been extremely illuminating for me; it had changed my life and probably even saved it. My credentials and the new job now positioned me to be the one behind the desk, providing therapy to others. And I loved it. At that early stage in my career, I struggled to maintain professional boundaries with employees, many of whom I'd partied with over the years, who still suffered from chemical dependency. I was tempted to over-identify with them: I had been them; they were me. I wanted to rescue them as I'd been rescued. But as it wound up, it wasn't only addicts that I was called upon to counsel. My subspecialty in crisis management was about to be moved from its sleepy, secondary position to being front, center, and urgent.

Pan Am's fatal blow as a viable airline arrived on December 21, 1988, when Flight #103, a Boeing 747 that Juan Trippe had helped design, departed on a regular route from Frankfurt to Detroit via London and New York. It exploded midair over Lockerbie, Scotland, when a 20" hole was punched in the fuselage by a bomb that had been placed in the aircraft hold. Within three seconds of the explosion, the nose of the plane sheared off. Shortly thereafter, on the ground fourteen miles away, the British Geological Survey registered a seismic event measuring 1.6 on the moment magnitude scale used by seismologists to measure earthquakes. This was the impact of the complete fuselage, incorporating the flight deck and nose landing gear, which was found in one hideous piece in a field approximately two and a half miles east of Lockerbie. The bomb had been hidden inside a tape recorder and then tucked into a suitcase, unbeknownst to the woman who had checked the bag prior to boarding the doomed flight. She was one of 243 passengers, 16 crewmembers, and 11 residents of Lockerbie on the ground that perished. Of the 270 total fatalities, 190 were American citizens, and 43 were British. Nineteen other nationalities were represented.

As manager of the EAP, I was immediately flown out of New York to London and then on to Lockerbie to coordinate all counseling services for Pan Am employees and their dependents. I had clinical experience as a psychologist, but my expertise in crisis psychology up to that moment was academic. I had no formal field training in what I was about to face.

Images of the plane, partially embedded in a field located opposite a church, with Flight #103's unmistakable blue and white nose, the name "Clipper Maid of the Seas" written in pretty blue letters across it, laid on its side, fully amputated from its body. This photograph appeared night after night on the news and in print media all over the world. The repeated imagery left the impression that flying Pan Am was now dangerous to your health and could, in fact, kill you. The company would not survive this disaster.

Libya eventually accepted responsibility for the terrorist attack and marked the first time any state sponsoring terrorism had compensated the terrorists' victims, to the tune of $10 million each. In exchange for this settlement, a deal was struck with the UN and the US, removing imposed sanctions and taking Libya off the State Department's list of countries financing terrorism. Some of the victims' families considered the deal blood money, and some families did not accept the payout at all because they believed Libya was innocent, having offered to pay the compensation as a tool to lift sanctions. Twenty-three years later, Tripoli would be held by rebel forces, Libya would fall, and Muammar Gaddafi—Libya's internationally condemned dictator whose administration violated human rights and had underwritten global terrorism—would be dead after forty-two years in power.

Just two years after the bomb took down Flight #103, the airline once associated with luxury, glamour, sophistication, and meteoric success filed for bankruptcy in January of 1991 and closed its doors on December 4 of that same year. Juan Trippe was saved from this heartbreak, having died ten years earlier of a stroke at age eighty-one. But the rest of us grieved the death of what had been a great iconic American success story and the sense of family that employment at Pan Am gave us all.

Pan Am's final flight, on April 4, 1991, was, just like the very first, out of Heathrow headed for New York. All employees on the ground in London gathered on the tarmac. Before taking off, the plane taxied through arcing water jets set up by the fire brigade. Once airborne, the plane circled back for a flyover, dipping its wings in a final bow, before disappearing forever, swallowed by a sky blue and broad, leaving no trace, almost as if the world was washed clean, untouched, and never written upon.

I, however, was indelibly marked. As a direct result of the Lockerbie tragedy, I now found myself forever altered. When I returned to New York, I became one of the "passionate pioneers" of the Air Transport Association (ATA), an industry trade and lobbying group developing aviation crisis management programs. I felt a great responsibility to my fellow airline colleagues to secure the best psychological crisis training available to mitigate the potential for secondary trauma caused when seeing, hearing, and being peripheral to a firsthand traumatic event happening to others. At the time, no such program existed. I took it upon myself; I felt it was my responsibility to marshal my energies and create a program not only for Pan Am but one that could be used throughout the entire industry. I wanted to spare others from the horrific experiences that I had had.

Working with traumatized and bereaved people can be a profoundly spiritual experience, and the power of prayer in surviving suffering is well-known. Mythology and all the great religions of the world are preoccupied with how the relationship between humanity and divinity is maintained in the face of human suffering. While psychological assistance along with bereavement counseling is essential in the aftermath of sudden death and trauma, it's imperative that clergy be available, too. When a death occurs, we look for answers from a variety of sources, whether spiritual, ecclesiastical, mystical or something else altogether. Traditionally, the priest, poet, and shaman—and more recently, the clinician—act as symbolic messengers of comfort and perspective when we have lost both.

I heard the calling, and its reverberation has held me enthralled ever since. For over thirty years now, I have followed this clarion call to somehow stem the pain of others. Whether the pain is caused by addiction, or the addiction is the salve to the pain, or triggered by an unspeakable disaster, or the result of childhood damage, the double helix of my calling is trauma combined with loss. Loss of life, loss of self-respect, loss of innocence, loss of freedom, control, choice, self. My own addiction was complicated by my genetic predisposition—alcoholism runs rampant throughout my ancestral lineage—and my unresolved childhood trauma. My alcoholism remained dormant until I lost myself in the bottom of a bottle while working for the airlines. Had that not happened, and had I not been working in that industry, I would not have been placed at the scene of the Lockerbie terrorist attack. As so many lives were shattered that day, mine suddenly snapped together to form a picture of what I must do and what my purpose was to be. Some call this "work." I call it my life. There was no choice but to follow.

Chapter III: In the Hands of the Saints

Although the world is full of suffering, it is also full of the over-coming of it.
　　—Helen Keller

Imagine walking into a clock shop, where a wide assortment of beautifully handcrafted, one-of-a-kind clocks are all keeping time. Mantle and carriage clocks, regulator, and grandfather clocks, no two alike, with pendulums gently swaying and counter-weights slowly descending. A greatly animated cacophony.

Now imagine all of them stilled at the exact same moment. This isn't muffled ticking or the chimes, bells, and cuckoo birds removed; this is hour and minute hands stopped, pendulums stopped, counter-weights stopped. The sudden silence would be deafening for just a moment. Try if you can to visualize this: in one fell swoop, 270 heartbeats stop. Among them are the heartbeats of tiny passengers whose lives had just begun: two 8-week-old babies, a 10-month-old, and a one-year-old. A toddler of 18 months and two 2-year-olds. A 3-year-old, a 5-year-old. Two 8-year-olds. A 9-year-old and three 10-year-olds. Other heartbeats that stopped: the excited-about-everything-all-the-time heartbeats of thirty-five students studying abroad from the University of Syracuse, including 20-year-old twin brothers. And, the wiser, more experienced heartbeats of a 76-year-old, a 79-year-old, an 81 and an 82-year-old, and every single generation in between represented more than once. A microcosm of the human lifespan was on Pan Am Flight

#103, comprised of every conceivable role by which we define ourselves: daughters, sons, mothers, fathers, sisters, brothers, husbands, wives, nieces, nephews, aunts, uncles, grandmothers, grandfathers. Friends, colleagues, lovers, single, married. Those still in swaddling blankets, the young, those in their prime, the aging, and the elderly. Preadolescents who would never reach adolescence. College students who would never wear a cap and gown. Teenagers, young adults, the middle-aged, those at the pinnacle of their careers, and those traveling in retirement. These aren't just words; these are people; these are, were, the passengers on that plane. Try to see them. All had hopes and dreams for themselves and for those they loved. All had been loved. All had had heartbeats that were stilled when all 270 of them were suddenly loosened and sent tumbling, spiraling, floating downward like so many angels evicted en masse from heaven. Inside the deafening explosion over Lockerbie, heartbeats silenced.

I lost a loved one on that flight. My good friend, Mary Geraldine Murphy, known as "Gerry," age fifty-one, was the "senior purser," or chief flight attendant, on board. Like me, she was from Ireland and was brought up in a large Catholic family. She had joined Pan Am in 1963 and generously shared her wealth of knowledge with all of us who came up through the ranks behind her. Mary held an honors degree in grief counseling and had graduated with a degree in social psychology. Based in London, our friendship grew when we were both at the professional standards association.

Immediately following the explosion, I was summoned to Lockerbie to coordinate the counseling services for the airline's employees, their families, and the families of the deceased passengers. I was on the same flight from New York to London as many of the victims' families. The flight felt like a flying wake. The first-class and coach cabins were both populated by grieving members of the victims' families, along with Pan Am employees who had been dispatched to Lockerbie to provide comfort and care. I was seated next to a young woman who had just lost her husband; she showed me pictures of her two young, now fatherless children. While I felt endless compassion for this new widow and suddenly single parent, I couldn't keep from being overwhelmed by imagining what lay ahead. If I wasn't completely present for the sobbing young woman next to me, how could I possibly be of help to the hundreds of others? It was my first time responding to an airline disaster, and I simply had no idea what I was to do.

Some of the early speculations about what had taken down the Lockerbie flight were based on the age of the plane—what's referred to as "metal fatigue." As our plane, of the same generation as Flight #103, bounced through continuous turbulence, those of us in the industry wondered if we too would suffer metal fatigue. The shock, sorrow, and disbelief of the tragedy were now overlaid with fear.

On Christmas Day, 1988, we were flown to Glasgow-Prestwick airport, where coach buses waited to drive us the eighty miles to Lockerbie. We were accompanied by howling winds, and rain drenched the roads to Lockerbie as it fell in an endless torrent from blackened skies. This weather was normal for Scotland in late December and perfectly mirrored how we were feeling. That ride from Prestwick airport to Lockerbie is permanently imprinted on my psyche, as clear and present as if it happened yesterday. The buses were filled with grieving family members and their fearful anticipation of the unknown, a universal hallmark of being catapulted into grief. I sensed that the return trip would be marked by a greater sense of calm and acceptance, as seeing the visual spot where loved ones had died can oftentimes provide the comfort of knowledge. Small comfort. This speculation proved to be accurate. On the return trip, the family members were exhausted yet calm as they presumably labored to integrate the faces of their lost loved ones with the images of the mangled remnants of the 747 aircraft strewn across the Scottish moors. Visually taking it all in, standing at the crash site can be a "severe mercy," kindness in the face of cruelty. Answering the questions of where and when, even when the how and why is still unknown, can be consoling.

As Lockerbie was my first aviation disaster, it was also the start of my work as an innovator of aviation crisis management, specifically from a psychological perspective. That perspective entails focusing on the psychological and emotional responses of the traumatized individual instead of simply conducting an administrative/tactical debriefing. Essentially, crisis management debriefing from a psychological perspective offers emotional first aid.

The fledging crisis response team we put together at Pan Am to better respond to the needs of the families of those lost on Flight #103 were not volunteers; all had been selected as "non-essential" airline employees and were assigned to provide care, comfort, and assistance, despite never formally being trained previously in grief counseling. We were a ragtag collection of airline personnel suddenly thrust into the role of caregiver during the most excruciating and intensely private moment in the lives of these families. And yet, despite the lack of preparation and professional training, this response team instinctively led from their hearts and gracefully carried the "human factor" aspects of the work at hand, including escorting the families and the remains of their loved ones home. We didn't follow our own self-care principles, which included adequate rest, proper nutrition, and the appropriate setting of personal boundaries, because we felt we had no right to personal comforts in the face of caring for those whose lives had suddenly been shattered. But the cost of not taking care of myself soon became due, and I was physically ill when I returned to London, which was the home base for the victims' families. Six weeks later, I returned to New York, spent physically, emotionally, spiritually, and extremely frustrated that we'd all faced this situation without training and proper preparation. After the Lockerbie disaster, I channeled my frustration into creating a professional crisis response program, just in case another disaster ever arrived. I spent the next three years developing curricula and resources within the Pan Am Employee Assistant Program.

In 1991, when Pan Am filed for bankruptcy protection, I left the company I'd loved so dearly and accepted the position of Director, Employee Assistance Program at TWA, Pan Am's nemesis in the race to own the skies back in the 50s and 60s. Juan Trippe and the brilliant, eccentric Howard Hughes, who owned a controlling share of TWA's stock, had battled it out for years in a competition of ingenuity, creativity, use of emerging technology and plain old gumption. By 1991 both, rest their souls, were competing from the grave.

In addition to many of the same responsibilities I'd held at Pan Am as the manager of their EAP, including counseling those with drug and alcohol addictions, my new duties included designing and implementing a disaster response program for TWA, just as I'd spent the last few years doing at Pan Am. Essentially, this new team was to take care of the grieving family members and anticipate their needs until identification and repatriation of their loved ones occurred. When the TWA executives asked how long it would take me to put together this program, I confidently told them three months. They laughed. But I had the sad blueprint and experience of having been baptized by fire at Lockerbie, and sure enough, the program launched in the Spring of 1992. One of the critical aspects of this program was to mitigate the risk of secondary trauma that airline employees might suffer in the aftermath of a disaster, as I had. I'd seen this up close and personally while working in Lockerbie and vowed to inoculate future airline personnel should they ever find themselves in the position we'd been in.

In 1995, with about a dozen other TWA staff personnel, I went to DC for disaster planning and next-of-kin notification training with US Army Colonel Michael Spinello, who had been awarded the Army Distinguished Service Medal for his work as Director, Casualty and Memorial Affairs[7]. Though notification to family members was not under my team's jurisdiction —that difficult work belonged to the reservations department in part due to their having so many employees, phone banks, and immediate access to passenger contact information—still, I felt that having the knowledge would benefit the team in terms of sensitivity, empathy, and understanding. Oddly, but certainly fortuitously, we were the only airline to accept the colonel's offer for training. Building this new program, we selected airline employees from both domestic and international divisions; 20 percent of TWA's volunteers were airline retirees[8]. They had been baggage carriers, ticketing agents, management, captains, and flight attendants. Those interested in volunteering were given special training and counseling services during and after deployment. The specialized training, recurring every year, included all practical aspects such as logistics, cultural awareness and sensitivity, appropriate language assignment, psychological insights, and the forensic aspects of identifying the deceased. I conducted this training with assistance from physicians, psychologists, clergy, and Colonel Spinello.

By midyear 1996, TWA had over six hundred trauma response team volunteers trained to respond to an aviation disaster. I was, affectionately, I believe, referred to as "The Disaster Queen." We were proud of each other and prayed that we would never be called to action. Our prayers were decisively unanswered on July 17, 1996, at 8:31 p.m. EDT.

"TWA Jetliner Leaving New York for Paris Crashes in Atlantic; More Than 220 Aboard"[9]

Exactly four minutes later, my phone rang. I was attending an annual summer conference at Pacifica Graduate Institute, near Santa Barbara, California, where I would receive my Doctorate of Philosophy in clinical psychology several years later. The call was from TWA's operations manager informing me that Flight #800 had disappeared from radar. I threw my belongings into my suitcase, and as I drove to the LA airport to board the first available flight back to New York, I knew from my experience in Lockerbie exactly what awaited me on the other side of the country. Unspeakable sorrow. Overwhelming helplessness. I knew I would feel a sense of déjà vu, and I most certainly did. What I'd been wrong about was thinking that Lockerbie would be my last airline disaster.

The explosion of TWA Flight #800 over Long Island Sound awakened the memories of my involvement with Pan American Flight #103. As I flew east, I was asking myself how it is that we come to accept such a tragedy and learn to cope with it? It seems to me that ours is a society that denies death: we have trouble talking about it in honest terms, speaking instead in metaphors and euphemisms, especially when talking to children. I have known people who had felt abandoned by their closest friends when they, or a close family member, had been diagnosed with a serious or terminal illness. These friends who stopped calling and making plans to get together later admitted to acting badly in the face of illness and death. They were so deeply uncomfortable that they sacrificed their friendship to stay within a comfort zone defined by denial. We tend to hide away our elderly and the ill, stealing ongoing connection from them with all they knew and loved, and pilfer wisdom, perspective and history from ourselves, our families, our communities, and society at large. We celebrate health, youth, and beauty, and we criticize our aging selves. We dishonor one another when the form begins to fade, when the hearing and the eyesight dim, when the gait becomes enfeebled. This disrespect for the natural process of living, giving way, in time, to dying, is endemic in our culture. How then do we make sense of death on such a large scale? How do we keep ourselves from being traumatized when tragedy strikes others? How do we talk about death, not only to those who have so suddenly lost their loved ones but how do we even talk to ourselves in moments like these? How do we not become hostages to death?

The passengers on this flight included young couples on their honeymoon, college kids, a high school French club and their chaperones, and people who had used their life savings to visit the romantic city of Paris. Memories of these crashes, these lost lives, are everlasting for me. Years later, I still feel great confusion and sadness. I simply cannot find an answer to why so many must die, why humanity is capable of such inhumanity, or why there is so much suffering.

Working with the traumatized is a privilege for me and one that I honor. I feel their souls are exposed, and we need to be prepared intellectually, emotionally, and spiritually to acknowledge that. As I sat on that endless flight from LA to New York as it flew through the night, I wondered if I was anywhere near prepared.

I arrived at the Ramada Plaza JFK Hotel, known as "Heartbreak Hotel" since it has housed families of victims of airline crashes in the 1990s and 2000s, at 7:30 a.m. on July 18. As director of the trauma response team and lead coordinator of the family assistance component for TWA, I'd been in touch with key members of the team while flying east, and by the time I reached the hotel, thirty team members were onsite and working with the earliest families to arrive. The response team had been well-trained organizationally, and hopefully, emotionally for the disaster, or as prepared as any human being can possibly be when faced with an immediate tragedy that has irrevocably altered the lives of hundreds, even thousands of people.

The ripple effect of airline disasters, and other community-wide tragedies such as school shootings and public space bombings, seeps and spreads to an astounding number of people. Our hearts break first for the shocking, senseless loss of life and the families and friends left behind. Others on the ground are forever changed as well: all of us who worked for TWA lost friends and colleagues; those on the front lines on the phones and at the ticketing counters dealing with the anguished family members desperate for information; the first responders called to the scene; the transit authority, coast guard and port authority personnel; the Red Cross and the other agencies that are immediately deployed; the last responders, the medical examiners, and coroners who face the daunting task of identifying the dead. While all are well-trained professionals adept at containing our emotions while performing the task at hand, all are also, and first, human beings. We are members of the same family, genus, and species; we are linked together so that when one falls, we all fall; when one suffers, we all suffer. It is impossible not to be touched and made more compassionate, more selfless, by the trauma of disaster.

Unless your name is Rudolph Giuliani. Mayor of New York City at the time, Giuliani and his staff descended on the scene like carrion-eating henchmen. Disruptive and callous don't begin to describe his persona. To several of us, he seemed hell-bent on politicizing this tragedy, anxious to be portrayed as the hero to the devastated families, especially when the news cameras were running. Since he directed his ire at my team, and specifically, at me, my read on him was that he was enraged and ashamed that the city didn't have a trained, prepared, and deployable trauma response team. I was one of the first TWA executives to arrive onsite after the plane went down. Perhaps Giuliani felt that the airline was responsible for the deaths of 230 people. Maybe he felt the airline whose plane had exploded over Long Island Sound, leaving not a single survivor, demonstrated the height of impropriety by having a presence at the hotel where the victims' families were gathered. Or maybe he had a problem with a strong woman directing the care and oversight of TWA's response team there. Perhaps he was keenly aware that as mayor, he'd let his constituents down badly by being so utterly ill-prepared for a tragedy of this magnitude. JFK sees a lot of passenger traffic, nearly 31 million people a year back in those years (nearly twice that now), with more than half flying internationally.[10] And yet the city had no human factor response plan in 1996 for a major aviation disaster.

Frankly, I didn't give a damn what Giuliani's reasons were. I found him and his staff contemptible and motivated by self-interest. When they bullied and eventually threatened to sue me if my team and I didn't vacate the premises, I ignored them. Nothing drives an egomaniac to the brink as quickly as being treated as if he's invisible, so that was the tactic I took with the mayor. My team and I held our ground, and we did our work. My hands were more than full from comforting the bereaved—six hundred family members had gathered at the Ramada—and my heart overflowed with sorrow. We offered what little consolation we could to the inconsolable. We took care of the myriad errands and logistics that every family has; we sat with them, shared meals with them, shielded them from the media and the politicians, and "held a space" for them to just be, to gather themselves, to feel safe in a newly realized unsafe world. A Portuguese poet of the last century, Fernando Pessoa, has a beautiful line in his poem titled "Discontinuous Poems," where he writes, "To be whole, it is enough to exist." I think of this when I "hold a space" for someone or for myself.

While post-disaster airline protocols have since changed, it's important to go back to how things were done in 1996 to understand the difficulties that ensued directly after the TWA explosion. One of the most frustrating, heart-wrenching ordeals to endure in the aftermath of an aviation disaster in that era was waiting for the definitive passenger manifest to be issued. There were iterative versions: the first one was produced hours before a departing flight to help flight attendants count special request meals, such as vegetarian or kosher offerings, and make accommodations for other specified requests. This was called a "spill list," and it'd be discarded once everyone was on board and the doors to the plane were closed, preventing a new passenger boarding or an existing one from getting off.[11] Only then was a final passenger manifest created. But still, circumstances can intervene, leaving room for error. If there's a connection or layover, a passenger, for any number of reasons, might not get back on board: perhaps he missed the boarding announcement, or she received an emergency call that instantaneously altered her plans, etc. As it was, there were two passengers who changed their plans at the very last moment and didn't board Flight #800 in New York. They arrived safe and soundly in Rome on another flight from a different airline; Rome had been the destination of Flight #800 after its scheduled stop in Paris. But neither had communicated the change of plans to their respective families, who, I can only imagine, suffered terribly thinking they had been on the doomed TWA flight.

While this complicated process of creating the last, definitive passenger manifest made practical sense, the wait feels nothing less than cruel to family members in the event of a disaster. In a crisis, nobody cares what the reasons or mitigating circumstances are that might delay the delivery of crucial information. We need answers when facing the unfathomable; we need to know if our loved one is safe, suffering or gone. The wait can feel interminable.

Giuliani had used the delay of the passenger list's availability as his own bully pulpit to the media. In his characteristically bombastic way, he'd been making demands of TWA officials to release the list, even though the passengers had not yet been verified. After staying at the hotel throughout the night of July 17, he left early the following morning to meet with television crews at three different news channels, where he ripped TWA and the vice president of airport operations up one side and down the other for "abandoning" the families of the deceased. It would take until 4:00 p.m. that day, twenty hours after the explosion, before a final passenger list was released. Giuliani and then-governor George Pataki rushed outside to be the first in front of the news cameras to deliver the "good" news, followed immediately by another Giuliani rant about how long it had taken TWA to provide a verifiable passenger manifest. What should have been a common goal between us wound up being at cross-purposes; what should have been a time to act with dignity and grace in honor of those who died was instead the opposite. But Giuliani is not a man generally known for being collaborative, tactful, or kind. TWA took heat from many quarters for this delay, and we took heat for not issuing a statement from headquarters immediately after the disaster. There were legitimate reasons and circumstances behind this, all moot in the face of six hundred grieving people. Those corporate imperatives didn't matter then, and they matter even less now, as wordy explanations never stem the pain. As one of the first TWA executives on the scene, I took the microphone in the ballroom at the Ramada when I arrived and said the only two words I thought might break through: "I'm sorry." These twenty-two years later, I still am so very, very sorry.

It's difficult to find adequate words to describe what last responders, the coroners, and medical examiners must contend with in the aftermath of an event that takes so many lives simultaneously. While prepared technically, psychologically and, presumably, emotionally for the work of identifying a victim and determining the how, where, and when of that death, imagine, in a heartbeat, having to deal with that times 230.

Blessedly, death usually comes quickly in an airline disaster. These deaths do not respect the wonder and beauty of the human form. On a hot summer day at the beach, you walk into the ocean gradually, and the water envelops you slowly. The wave comes in as a swell and splashes you from ankle to shin; then, as you walk forward, from shin to knee, from knee to thigh to waist to chest and then you float on the surface, buoyed and supported by the very stuff we're all made of. The human body is 60 percent water; certain organs, such as the heart, brain, and lungs, are more than 80 percent water. The ocean laps at us in an organic, deeply familiar way. Despite its vastness, regardless of the height of waves or the pull of tides, it has always felt more friend than foe to me. There's a comfort and a peace it instills in my very soul, and I feel it every time I walk the beach.

But if not entered slowly, if instead one is slammed onto it from above, the form changes from liquid to solid, and solid in the most unforgiving way. It will fragment what falls onto it. In one striking exception, the police boats recovered one of the TWA pilots, golden wings still pinned to his uniform breast pocket. An officer on that boat reported that the pilot appeared as if sleeping peacefully on the surface of the oil-slicked water, with no evidence of the trauma that had brought him there.[12] This can be even more unnerving for responders than the morbid task of collecting shattered remains because it deviates from expectation and defies logic. "He looked perfect," and yet was still gone. By the time the pilot was retrieved, the responders were sure there would be no survivors. They were right.

My work as a crisis manager in New York was not limited to the families and the airline employees on the ground; it extended to these first and last responders as well. Their task was overwhelming, and the pressure placed on them to retrieve and quickly identify bodies was enormous. Most had no experience with the kind of physical devastation impact a hard surface makes on a body. I remember standing in front of a large bulletin board in the administrative and identification processing office, trying to make sense of the photographs pinned to it. Then the gravity of the crash seared into me in a way the busyness of my work there hadn't yet allowed. I stood there numb, swaying on my feet; I felt outside myself, outside reality. So many faces, so many lives suddenly gone, now displayed as necessary pieces of a terrible forensic puzzle. We might be able to imagine it and read about it in training, but seeing it within the context of 230 lost lives is something else altogether.

President Clinton and First Lady Hillary Rodham Clinton arrived in New York a full week after the disaster and only after receiving a tsunami of criticism for being so late. Bill Clinton was known as "mourner-in-chief" because of his prominent appearance at numerous funerals in the Spring of that year, including that of Commerce Secretary Ron Brown, a close friend and federal appointee who died in a Croatian plane crash, Admiral Jeremy Boorda, head of the Navy, and at two memorial services in late June for military victims of the Saudi Arabia terrorist truck bomb. In April of 1995, Clinton attended the first anniversary of the bombing at the Alfred P. Murrah Federal Building in Oklahoma City. It was painful and confusing to the families as to why his arrival in New York appeared to be such an afterthought. Upon finally getting to The Ramada, the Clintons were first briefed on the status of the salvage operation before meeting privately for a couple of hours with the families of the victims. Clinton had apparently left the official role to Governor Pataki and Mayor Giuliani, who I and others felt had grossly mishandled the disaster. But Clinton's eventual presence there would make a strong impression on him and the First Lady, and that impression would soon influence the legal protocols in the immediate aftermath of future airline disasters.[13]

Hillary Clinton also met personally with the families and TWA employees who were responding to the disaster. I had an opportunity to brief Mrs. Clinton about the duties of my team as I escorted her, along with several secret service personnel, to the conference room we used as our headquarters. During the short walk down the hallway, I had the distinct impression that Mrs. Clinton wasn't listening to a word I said. But as she began to address the TWA employees at the makeshift podium, she repeated verbatim every word I had included in my briefing. I was truly impressed.

Where there's a void, desperation to fill it floods in. Several theories, including a conspiracy that the US government had covered up the true cause of the explosion, were circulated at the time. In the first hours after the explosion, terrorism was suspected in the form of either an on-flight bomb or a missile strike. But as the deceased were recovered and inspected, and as pieces and parts of the plane were collected and analyzed, there was no evidence a high-impact explosion of that type had occurred. Trace amounts of explosive residue were discovered in the wreckage, but that was later found to likely be cross-contamination from military personnel during and after the recovery operation. It was also possible the plane might have been used as a test site for bomb-sniffing dogs prior to the accident, but that too was never proven—or unproven—it simply remained a possibility.

It took until August 23, 2000, a full four years and five weeks after the explosion of Flight #800, for the National Transportation Safety Board (NTSB) to conclude its investigation and issue the final report on what had likely caused the plane to explode twelve minutes after takeoff. In part, the NTSB final report stated the following:

> The probable cause of the TWA flight 800 accident was an explosion of the center wing fuel tank (CWT), resulting from ignition of the flammable fuel/air mixture in the tank. The source of ignition energy for the explosion could not be determined with certainty, but of the sources evaluated by the investigation, the most likely was a short circuit outside of the CWT that allowed excessive voltage to enter it through electrical wiring associated with the fuel quantity indication system. Contributing factors to the accident were the design and certification concept that fuel tank explosions could be prevented solely by precluding all ignition sources..."[14]

The report is thorough and yet ultimately inconclusive; conclusions were drawn more by disqualifying causes than by finding a definitive smoking gun. This can be very frustrating, especially for the families of the deceased, but this lack of certainty is common. The causes of some accidents are clear, like a sheared bolt or metal fatigue causing an in-flight breakup. Other accidents are at best a guess, even after months if not years of investigation. And so it was in the case of TWA Flight #800. We will never know with certainty what caused that explosion.

During its investigation and in its final report, the NTSB issued fifteen safety recommendations, mostly covering fuel tank and wiring-related issues. Among the recommendations for new (and, where feasible, existing) planes was the development of modifications such as nitrogen-inerting systems, which would decrease the likelihood of combustion in a confined space by maintaining inert nitrogen gas. This led the FAA to propose a ruling requiring the same, which was finally adopted in July 2008, eight years after the NTSB issued its final report on Flight #800.

As a result of the chaotic aftermath of the disaster, including TWA's sluggish response to the victims' families, turf wars between the county, city, state, and federal agencies involved in the investigation, the posturing and politicization Giuliani had employed, and the competing agendas between the FBI and the NTSB, material and meaningful changes came about to better serve the families of airline disasters. The Air Transportation Association, an industry group, presented the Aviation Disaster Family Assistance Act. And just two months after Flight #800 went down, President Clinton signed an executive order making the NTSB, not the airlines or the FBI, responsible for managing the needs of the victims' families. This centralized activities, streamlined operations, and created greater objectivity.

The Act was also intended to prevent future catastrophes from being used as exploitive leverage, as it prevented lawyers, politicians, and other parties from contacting family members for thirty days after an airline disaster. A month later, in October of 1996, Congress made the Act law. President Clinton may have been late to initially show up, but he was quick to act to correct what he had seen. He had experienced for himself the anguish all that dysfunction and self-serving had wrought, and he did something permanent about it.

But in July, the benefits of that were all in the future. The only future the families of those on board Flight #800 might have been thinking about was how in the world they were going to face theirs without their loved one. They were simply trying to place one foot in front of the other while they waited first for the passenger manifest, then for the deceased to be retrieved, then to be identified, and then for the body to be released to the family. Only then could they think about going home. Home: our place of healing, safety, and sanctuary. Until the families could go home, all were left in a state of suspended animation.

As a result of these two airline disasters, I experienced what I can only call a mystical awakening. Whether in a conference room at JFK, a hotel in London, or in a community center in Lockerbie, strangers of all ages, nationalities, races, and belief systems, all now members of a makeshift community suddenly born from death, expressed a real love and compassion for one another. Boundaries, which usually serve to maintain a "safe distance" from the unknown, were shed instantaneously: people who hadn't known each other hours before were now embracing and providing shelter for one another. Hands were held, backs patted, and tears gently wiped away before falling again, in the intimacy that comforting brought forth even when names hadn't yet been exchanged. Utter vulnerability, an element so primitive and raw, was revealed in front of my eyes. For me, it was an affirmation of a sublime presence in the universe.

These tragedies have transformed me, and even now, I have reflective moments of the profoundly personal experiences I had while working with the victims' families. The losses somehow make my heart larger, my soul deeper; I think this is what we sometimes refer to as a "spiritual" experience. I recall one woman who affected me in this way. She had just lost her daughter on Flight #800, and as we were departing the hotel to attend the memorial service, she asked if she could accompany me to hangar 12, where the memorial was being held. I said of course, and together we climbed into a Port Authority police car to transport us there. As we made our way, she told me her story: her daughter had been a young student traveling alone to Paris, where she was going to study French. She then turned to me and beseechingly asked if her daughter had suffered when the plane exploded. I recall that moment and what it felt like viscerally and physically as if it was just yesterday. Suddenly nothing else in the world existed or mattered. There was no light, no shadow; there was no sound of the car's tires rotating on the pavement or the sound of the driver breathing. It was a crystalline moment suspended in time and space, where one woman turned to another, seeking an answer that might save her, give her some peace, or some semblance of peace or deliverance. I was physically and emotionally exhausted and yet suddenly keenly alert to a sense of gravitas, or grace, not in or from me, but through me. When I told her I could assure her, with absolute certainty, that her child had not suffered, she looked at me with wide, dubious eyes. I explained that the uncontrolled decompression, followed by an in-flight breakup at high speed, would have created such intense g-forces that all on board would have been immediately rendered unconscious. Her daughter never knew what happened; she had no foresight, no fear, and no pain. In the seconds that followed my answer, I heard the beating of our hearts, and with our eyes locked onto one another's, I was aware that each of our lives had suddenly clicked forward a gear. I don't know how else to explain this other than to call it a spiritual experience.

Bearing witness at the Ramada was Father Mychal Judge, a Franciscan friar and Catholic priest who served as chaplain to the New York Fire Department (NYFD). He had volunteered to assist us in counseling the family members and the TWA employees. He was a selfless man, giving himself freely to all who were in need, and he had a special place in his heart for the underserved, underrepresented, and misunderstood. He ministered to the homeless, the hungry, the addicted, those suffering from AIDS, immigrants, gays and lesbians, and those alienated by the church and society at large. As a child, he'd been greatly influenced by the friars at the church, St. Francis of Assisi, across the street from where he and his family lived. He later said that watching the friars in the church made him want to join them. He began his formation process at the age of fifteen, and years later, at fifty-three, he was assigned to the very same church that had originally inspired him. He had become the man his child self had wanted to be. Literally and figuratively, he came home.

Many representatives from different religious denominations assisted us at the Ramada Hotel, and we deeply appreciated every one of them. But the feelings Father Judge inspired in others were on a different level altogether. His essence was undeniable. He volunteered to stay with us for several weeks, comforting family members and TWA employees. I'd heard my fellow workers speaking fondly about Father Judge for days, but I hadn't had a chance to sit down and visit with him personally. On a Sunday two weeks after the crash, he and I finally arranged to meet in the hotel's garden. Every evening, the TWA staff and family members who wished to join us gathered there for prayers, usually led by clergy. We had turned this garden into an impromptu sacred space, a kind of Zen sanctuary. It became a refuge for grief and a respite from the chaos. Father Judge and I finally sat down together there that Sunday afternoon. We immediately discovered many things we had in common: he had been born in Brooklyn to parents who'd immigrated from Ireland, so we shared a common heritage. He had begun his recovery from alcoholism in 1971, around the same time my addiction was blossoming. With the help of his recovery program, he, like me, continued to speak about his addiction and help those who also suffered. We were both spiritual seekers. As we talked, I came to understand why he was so beloved among the TWA staff. His authenticity, humility, and sense of humor utterly captivated me, and that day in the garden, we became fast friends. Before we parted, he gave me a set of rosary beads that had been blessed by the Pope. It remains one of my most precious possessions, and after 9/11, I had it made into a bracelet that I wear to this day, especially and always when working in the aftermath of disasters.

Although spiritual growth is a type of healing from which many of us benefit, the one who is suffering may question the purpose of spirituality immediately following a traumatic event. We may question the existence of God and the purpose of our own lives. Into the hole left behind by loss, everything once felt to be meaningful can drop, sink, and drown. And yet, "The wound is the place where the light enters you," wrote Rumi, the thirteenth-century poet and mystic. I believe these are among the truest words I know.

This belief is founded on my own life's journey and from being witness to the pain of countless others through these aviation disasters, my addiction counseling practice, my consulting work with first and last responders, and my own family members, friends, and community. I don't know why it is, but it seems we must break before we can be made whole.

The potential for spiritual growth may expand at any time in life, and I've certainly seen this as we age. As the years tick by, we hopefully experience life at a deeper level. The deeper we feel love and joy, the corresponding loss and grief strike us deeper as well. The depth of pain can place us on a path of seeking spiritual comfort. This expansion can also take hold in the wake of sudden and devastating loss. In her book *Finding Beauty in a Broken World*, author Terry Tempest Williams, a naturalist and biologist, writes, "A mosaic is a conversation between what is broken." I love that; it's a beautiful phrase that captures my belief that we're made whole by the excruciating process of first being shattered. The irony is not lost on me that as lives are destroyed in the event of a disaster, through childhood trauma, or through the slow fracturing and pulling apart caused by addictions, we can be rent asunder and yet form whole again through that very process. What breaks our hearts can also heal them. I don't mean to sound Pollyannaish here or to minimize or turn away from the pain. I believe that "being in" that pain is crucial, for however long that takes. What I'm trying to express is that for some, and for me, the pain can give way to something else. Something that is both less than it was before it broke, but also larger, deeper, accompanied by a sense of connection to something outside ourselves. It's possible to find a source of comfort carried by the wind, in birdsong, in the belly laugh of a year-old child that we've seen and heard a million times before but only now is somehow listened to anew. Put another way, it's a willingness, however unconscious, to find beauty in the world, to find purpose, to feel alive again. This is how we survive trauma. This is how we survive, period.

Five years after meeting him in the aftermath of Flight #800's demise, on September 11, 2001, my friend, Father Mychal Judge, would die while in service to others. Upon hearing of the attack, he had rushed to the scene of the World Trade Center and was praying over the bodies of the injured and dead in the lobby of the North Tower when the second plane hit the South Tower. Debris from the second strike flew through the lobby of the North Tower, killing Father Judge and many others instantly. His was the very first certified death on September 11. While many had died before him, including those on United Flight #93, which went down in a field in rural Pennsylvania, and those on the planes that flew into both towers of the World Trade Center and the Pentagon, Father Mychal Judge was designated as "Victim 0001" because his was the first body to be recovered and taken to the medical examiner. A lieutenant of the NYPD, two firemen, an emergency medical technician, and a civilian carried his body out of the ruins; a Reuters photographer captured the moment, and that image became one of the most poignant testaments of 9/11. The *Philadelphia Weekly* referred to the photo as an "American Pietà," which is a subject in Christian art depicting the Virgin Mary holding the body of Jesus, such as the famous marble sculpture by Michelangelo that resides at St. Peter's Basilica in the Vatican City.

Even before his death, many referred to Father Mychal as a living saint because of his selfless charitable work and his deep spirituality. After his death on 9/11, people in the Roman Catholic Church called for him to be canonized, and on July 27, 2002, the Orthodox Catholic Church of America bestowed upon him the name of Saint Mychal Judge or Saint Mychal the Martyr.

I had been called back to New York in the immediate wake of the September 11th terrorist attacks. At the time, I was living in St. Louis and working as director of the EAP and disaster response teams at TWA's corporate headquarters. As I entered the building early that morning, I was distracted by many of my co-workers gathered around a large TV mounted on the lobby wall. Just moments before, the first plane had flown directly into the World Trade Centers. Our immediate reaction was concern that it had been a TWA plane because we knew that would mean an urgent deployment of activities outside the norm. None of us yet realized the full scope of what we were seeing.

There were seventeen minutes between the first plane hitting the North Tower and the second plane striking floors 77 through 85 of the South Tower, seventeen minutes in which life as we all knew it still bore a resemblance to a familiar world of possibilities and logic. Perhaps this was a tragic accident? A mechanical failure, or perhaps a "bird strike," one of those rare occurrences when a bird hits the jet engine? But upon the arrival of minute eighteen, that resemblance to a familiar world shattered.

Before the South Tower was hit, I had gone up to my office to take a call from American Airlines. I was being asked to get to New York City as quickly as possible to help the airlines and crew deal with what had just happened. At the time that call came in, American Airlines Flight #11 was the only air disaster that morning. But seventeen minutes later, it was United Flight #175 that struck the South Tower, and while on the phone with American, my other lines lit up, blinking insistent red beacons. Red as in emergency, red as in danger, red as in the life force coursing through our veins and now spilled. American and United each lost two aircraft that day. American Flight #77 slammed into the Pentagon thirty-four minutes after the second tower was hit, and United's Flight #93, detoured by rebel heroes on board from its rumored White House target, crashed into a field in rural Pennsylvania twenty-six minutes later. I was asked to immediately fly to New York, but I couldn't; nobody could fly anywhere. In an unprecedented move, all aircraft were immediately grounded; flights already underway were redirected to land at the closest possible airport. Nobody knew anything other than the country seemed to be under a murderously efficient siege, with commercial aircraft being used as artillery. At the airport in the small town of Gander, Newfoundland, thirty-eight wide-bodied transatlantic flights suddenly landed, and for the nearly 7000 people from numerous countries aboard those flights, this tiny outpost would become "home" until the US reopened its airspace three days later. The little town had fewer than 10,000 residents that year, but the townsfolk and those of the surrounding fishing villages placed cots in all their churches, schools, and community centers for the freshly stranded, some of whom were hosted in the private homes of the residents. Bus drivers, who'd been on strike that day, went back to work. Bakeries baked around the clock, and the mayor of a nearby town cooked elaborate meals with help from many of his townspeople. Along with the "plane people," the unexpected visitors included seventeen domestic pets and, oddly, two great apes, all of whom were given shelter, food, and love.

At the end of this unanticipated stopover, none of the townspeople of Gander or the surrounding villages would accept payment for their kindness. One of the "plane people", an eighty-year-old long-time fund-raiser at Ohio State University by the name of Shirley Brooks-Jones, who had been on her way home from Europe on 9/11, started a collection among her fellow passengers the day they were allowed to depart. By the time she landed back home, she'd raised $15,000 for a scholarship program for the children of Gander. Unbeknownst to her at the time, the captain had informed his fellow pilots about her campaign, and a fund-raising campaign rolled out on all thirty-eight planes that had been grounded in Gander. The "Lewisporte Area Flight 15 Scholarship Fund" (previously known as "Gander Flight 15 Scholarship Fund") raised more than $2 million by 2016. One of the students who received a scholarship went on to medical school and returned to Gander as a town doctor. The remarkable story of this town, its people and their 7000 unexpected guests has been made into a Tony-award-winning Broadway play titled *Come from Away*, a reference to local vernacular describing where outsiders are from —they are "from away."[15]

Unable to fly on 9/11, my colleague and dear friend, Ellyn Kravette, and I drove the fourteen hours straight through from St. Louis to the eastern seaboard. Ellyn had just learned that her son-in-law, who had been with the NYFD, had been killed in the attack, and it was in that car that my cell phone rang with the news from my friend, Captain Arikian, that Father Mychal Judge had just died. This unfathomable event nearly 1,000 miles away was magnified and made excruciatingly personal within the small space of our car. Ellyn and I had been friends for many years and had shared many experiences together; our familiarity with one another created a safe place for both of us as we cried our way across the country. Reflecting on that road trip, I still cannot find words that adequately describe the state we were in. I know I kept my foot on the accelerator and my hands on the wheel, but I don't know where the rest of me was. My mind was reeling, and yet I had no coherent thoughts. My heart was beating, but the blood felt frozen in my veins. My tongue was thick, my throat dry. I don't remember anything we talked about or if I ever spoke a word. If we gave each other comfort, it was simply by not being alone. The horror of what happened that day had been so difficult to wrap my mind around, but now suddenly, the impact of it slammed into me, becoming intensely personal. We were two stunned, mute creatures sitting in the same post-apocalyptic space, traveling through time and miles to misery and heartbreak that our world, Ellyn's and mine, could only mimic. I lost Father Mychal; Ellyn lost her son-in-law, whom she loved dearly, and she now had the heart-wrenching years-long work ahead of trying to comfort her devastated daughter. And yet it felt as if our losses were a pale comparison to what I knew was at the end of this road trip. I lost a dear friend, not a son, husband, or brother. Ellyn's loss was likewise one degree removed. But how do you compare one pain against another, one broken heart against someone else's? This seems to be a distinction without a difference, an impossible measure to take. The enormity of the personal losses and atrocity of bombed-out Lower Manhattan, the skeletal steel framework of the towers mangled and torqued and yet in part still standing, though barely, as if held up by gossamer. I tried to imagine what lay ahead, and it made my own suffering feel almost self-indulgent. This thought only brought a fresh swell of tears. I couldn't talk myself into or out of anything I was feeling.

I dropped Ellyn off in Newark to join her daughter, and by the time I got to New York, that car ride would pretty much be the last time I'd sit down for the next month. My sixteen–eighteen-hour workdays once there left time for nothing but the stolen hours of sleep.

My days there centered around the airline employees, crew members and ground personnel, all of whom were shell-shocked by grief, disbelief, and the effects of secondary trauma. More than one told me that while getting onto the subway near Ground Zero as they headed to work the morning of the attacks, they saw bodies falling from the sky thick with billowing thunderheads of ash and smoke. How does anyone make sense of that? What can anyone possibly say in response? What good could I, or anyone, possibly do? After air travel resumed, several flight attendants shared with us that they had drawn up their wills, now suddenly terrified to fly. Having once stood in their shoes, I knew that every wave of turbulence would now be perceived as their death knell. One young flight attendant shared with me that she was afraid to fly and believed that the terrorist attacks happened because we were removing prayers from the schools, becoming a Godless country. These are manifestations of secondary trauma, and whether rational or not, represent the effort we go through to make sense out of the senseless, looking for safety when we've just experienced the randomness of death. My work called upon me to somehow find internal resources to respond with compassion, understanding, and patience, even when I felt devoid of all those feelings. I remember saying to that young woman that we all had a loving God and that she was going to be protected on her flight. I gave her a visual image to focus on. I encouraged her to imagine being surrounded by angels (or any type of spiritual guide she might have resonated with) and to imagine them surrounding her aircraft and all the other planes in the sky. In my work there, I used all words of comfort I could find and tried to figure out who needed what. Visuals of angels might not have comforted a coroner, FBI agent or a skeptic of Christianity's use of angelic symbolism to depict God being close at hand, but it may have helped this young, frightened flight attendant. She went back to work 30,000 feet up in the sky, surrounded by her winged guides who, she believed, offered her safe passage.

For many years, I'd been associated with The International Critical Incident Stress Foundation (ICISF), also known as CISM (Critical Incident Stress Management). It is a method of helping first responders and others deal with the emotional and physical after-effects of their involvement with critical (traumatic) events. Its highly effective methodology has been used for first responders since 1983 and was adopted by the airlines in 1992 to assist pilots and flight attendants who experience a disaster. I'm certified to teach both basic and advanced critical incident stress debriefings, but when the New York Transit Authority (NYTA) contacted me ten days after I arrived in New York, wanting me to teach their employees the skills necessary to assist in debriefings, I think I actually screamed into the phone. My "Hell NO!" reply belied my total physical and emotional exhaustion. I was wrung out and empty; I had nothing to offer. I knew I was the only one qualified to conduct the training, given my certification and past experiences in Lockerbie and with TWA Flight #800. Additionally, I was up-to-date on all airline rules and regulations. But I was beyond spent. My persuasive friend and colleague, TWA Captain Greg Arikian of the Air Line Pilots Association, did his best to change my mind, promising me his help if I said yes. With pressure mounting on all sides, I think it was my utter fatigue, not my better angels, that caused me to capitulate.

The NYTA headquarters was in Brooklyn; from the windows there, we watched as smoke endlessly poured from the ruins of the World Trade Center. It would take a hundred days after the attack for all the fires surrounding Ground Zero to be extinguished. Arikian and I trained sixty individuals on the CISM debriefing methodology. Once trained, these foot soldiers could return to Ground Zero and provide an informed type of aid in mitigating stress and establishing coping mechanisms for the Port Authority rescue workers employed there.

I am often asked how responding to 9/11 was different than Lockerbie and Flight #800; were the physical, emotional, psychological, and spiritual consequences the same or different from those other disasters? In each case, my job was to respond in the capacity of a mental health professional, and the responsibilities and demands placed on me were the same. But the difference between 9/11 and my previous experience was one of magnitude, coupled with a sense of suspended reality. In Lockerbie and in New York, right after Flight #800 exploded in the sky, we had immediate help at our disposal. When an aviation disaster occurs, there are myriad local and national resources that immediately descend: trained family assistance employees of the airlines, the Red Cross, victims' assistance representatives, chaplains and rabbis, and police to protect the integrity of the "inner sanctum" where the grieving next-of-kin are secluded. At both Lockerbie and on Long Island Sound in the immediate aftermath of Flight #800, there was no shortage of resources deployed. But everything we'd been trained to expect in terms of support after an airline disaster was utterly suspended for the first several days after the attacks of 9/11. All aircraft had been grounded; there was no precedent for the world standing still as if paralyzed. Everything we could previously count on and lean into after a disaster was suddenly gone. Our reliance was on local resources exclusively, all of whom were stretched beyond the maximum. First responders, mental health professionals, clergy, and agency representatives all had to drive in from locations far outside the city. The skies were empty, but the roads were choked. And the scope of this disaster was beyond measure: it seemed that everyone in New York knew someone who had died in the Twin Towers. Everywhere I went—the airport, hotel, inside a taxi—everyone I interacted with either knew someone who had lost a loved one or had lost someone themselves. The scale of 9/11 was astronomical; it blew a hole in the entire universe. Three days after the attacks, I walked to Ground Zero and stood alongside the newly erected chain link fence, looking uncomprehendingly at the debris and chaos. My heart ached as I watched the workers. Some of the police officers and firefighters looked so young and confused that I wanted to reach out and hold them. Their shepherd and my friend, Father Mychal Judge, had been taken from them when they needed him the most, and I couldn't begin to fill his shoes. All I could do was to stand witness and hope that they felt the presence of spiritual love I was channeling in their direction.

As a psychologist, I knew it was an impossibility to be both emotional and cognitive simultaneously. My job with the first and last responders of 9/11 was seated in the cognitive realm, and I simply had to compartmentalize and defer my emotions until the completion of my task. It was only after I returned to my home in St. Louis about a month later that the emotions I had suspended emerged and rocked my world like an earthquake of the soul. I literally could hardly get out of bed, shower, or dress, let alone leave the house for groceries.

My deepest distress is in trying to assimilate man's inhumanity to man, questioning if anything makes sense or if all suffering is useless. While the steps are slow for me, I seek comfort in a psychological, philosophical, and spiritual orientation. I look to the masters of thought, religion, literature, and art to help me accept and eventually integrate these devastating experiences into my life. From the safety of finally returning to my own home, I looked within myself and to those thought leaders gone before to find ways to mend this wounded healer.

Photos

Thatched-roofed farmhouses of old Ireland.

This is the now remodeled house where all nine of us lived: six children, my parents and Uncle Joe ... without the benefit of plumbing or electricity.

The River Laune, in my hometown of Killorglin.

The old eight-arch Killorglin Bridge, built in 1885, still spans the Laune River. Both photos courtesy of Esther Leahy.

The pilgrimage trail and view from Mount Brandon.

My parents Tom and Molly Sullivan, circa 1939.

Left to right: sister Kathleen, mother Molly, me and brother Patrick, 1954.

My father arm-in-arm with my sister Eileen at her wedding in 1967, with sister Kathleen standing by.

Sisters Eileen and Bridget, circa 1960.

Previously known as the County Hospital of Killarney, where I spent three months of my 11th year.

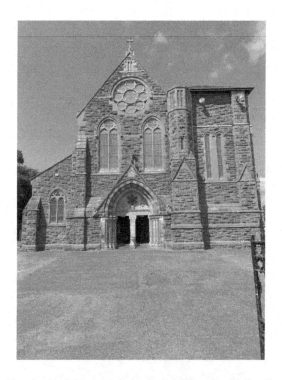

St. James Church, the Catholic church of my childhood in Killorglin. Photo courtesy of Esther Leahy.

Iconic Pan Am stewardesses, circa 1960's.

The Pan Am crews' uniforms in this era were conceived by Edith Head, who won a record 8 Academy Awards for costume design, making her the most awarded woman in the Academy's history.

Pan Am "Yankee Clipper" Flight #101 brought The Beatles to America for the first time in February 1964. The company was way ahead of its time in the use of product placement and staging celebrities to advance the brand.

Graduation from Pan Am inflight academy 1970; I'm in the 2nd row, 5th from left.

I'm on the far left with my cabin cohorts.

The glamour shot by Francesco Scavullo, used by Pan Am for their international magazine.

I'm on the far left.

The party girl most definitely out of uniform.

The United Nations Chapel where Sean and I married in May 1980.

My best man, brother Patrick.

Once we were young: me and Sean.

Gerry Murphy
Purser
Joined Pan Am March 4, 1963

My friend, fellow Irish lass and mentor, Mary "Gerry" Murphy, one of 270 who perished on December 21, 1988.

The devastated town of Lockerbie and the giant crater blown into the ground when Pan Am Flight #103 exploded.

The flight deck of Pan Am Flight #103, "The Clipper of the Sea" where it landed three miles outside of Lockerbie, part of a 70-mile wake of wreckage. (Photo courtesy of the British Air Accident Investigation Branch.)

An example of what the doomed TWA Flight #800 looked like upon liftoff out of JFK Airport on July 17, 1996. (Photo courtesy of Mark L. Berry.)

"Heartbreak Hotel" at JFK Airport, where the families of those lost on TWA Flight #800 were housed during the insufferable wait to be reunited with their lost loved ones. A week after the tragedy, the Clintons finally arrived. The Ramada still stands, though it ceased operations in 2009.

My friend Father Mychal Judge. We first met in the immediate aftermath of the explosion of TWA Flight #800 over Long Island Sound, and developed an immediate and deep connection while working together there. I still wear the rosary he gave me in the garden area of the "Heartbreak Hotel;" he is with me always.

The reconstruction of TWA Flight #800, a painstaking effort to determine the cause of the explosion. Comprised of more than 1600 pieces recovered from Long Island Sound, measuring 93 feet and weighing 60,000 pounds, it was announced in July 2021 that the wreckage would be destroyed, 25 years after the tragedy.

Brothers in arms, mugging for all cameras: then mayor Rudy Giuliani and then governor George Pataki.

New York City September 11, 2001.

New York City September 11, 2001.

Father Mychal Judge, gently carried by first responders. Serving as a chaplain to the NYC Fire Department, he was offering aid and prayers to the rescuers, the injured and the dead in the lobby of the North Tower. When the South Tower collapsed, sending debris flying through the North Tower lobby, he was killed instantly. His death was designated as "Victim 0001."

"First From the Flames" memorial statue by Timothy P. Schmalz, of the 9/11 firefighters carrying Father Judge out of the North Tower wreckage.

My dear friend Ellyn Kravette, who drove with me from St. Louis to New York City on 9/11/2001.

The Betty Ford Center, Rancho Mirage, California where I served as VP of Treatment Services 2006 – 2013.

With Susan Ford-Bales, the youngest child of President and First Lady Ford, and Chair of the Betty Ford Center, circa 2007.

The Las Vegas Recovery Center.

Giving a tour of the residential quarters while serving as CEO 2013 – 2015.

Pacifica Graduate Institute in Carpenteria, California, where I received my Doctorate in Clinical Psychology.

My sister Kathleen came from Germany to commemorate my graduation in 2005.

Pacifica's beautiful campus.

The Wardholme Torrey Pine, the tallest in the world at 126 feet high, 20 foot circumference and a branch width of 130 feet, in downtown Carpenteria. Its stature always reminded me of the tallest of the 14 crosses marking the Mount Brandon pilgrimage trail near my hometown of Killorglin.

The Mandalay Bay Hotel, where Stephen Paddock opened fire on the evening of October 1, 2017 from his 32nd floor suites, firing more than 1000 bullets into the crowd of the Route 91 Harvest Music Festival below...

... sending the attendees running for their lives. Before the nightmare ended, Paddock killed 60 individuals and injured 867 more.

I had just arrived in Dallas to give a presentation to American Airlines when I received the call to return immediately to Las Vegas the night of the shooting.

Working with members of the Las Vegas Fire Department.

Working with the Blackfoot Chemical Dependency Program, 1991.

Poster for the 1999 documentary of the Alkali Lake community and its journey to sobriety and reconciliation.

Renderings of the Irish Hedge Schools.

Family reunion in England, 2003. Top row left to right: Maureen, Patrick and Bridget. Bottom row, left to right: Eileen, me and Kathleen.

With the memorial to Monsignor O'Flaherty (1898–1963) in Killarney, 2015. He was an Irish Catholic priest and significant figure of resistance to the Nazi occupation, credited with saving 6500 Allied soldiers and Jews. He was also my husband Sean's cousin.

With cousin Pat Bowler.

My cousin Denis Bowler and Esther Bowler Leahy, Killarney 2015.

The extended Bowler clan at our 2016 reunion in Killarney.

My sister Bridget and King Puck who is honored annually at the Puck Fair Festival. The festival dates back to 1613, but the statue wasn't installed until long after our childhoods in Killorglin ended.

Family reunion 2016. Top row left to right: Maureen, Patrick and Bridget. Bottom row, left to right: Eileen, me and Kathleen.

Dr. Andrea Barthwell, past president of the American Society of Addiction Medicine (ASAM), my great friend and keynote speaker Judy Collins, and me at the 2018 ASAM convention in San Diego.

Giving a presentation at the University of Las Vegas, 2019.

At rest and at peace, and after all the years, feeling at home in Ireland, 2000.

Jordan, 2000, where I was hired to facilitate human factor training for Royal Jordananian Airlines.

Top left: Pan Am Flight #103, Lockerbie 1988. Bottom left: same location 2018. Top right: crash debris 1988. Bottom right: same location 2018.

Memorial in the rebuilt town of Lockerbie 2018.

The mangled "forgotten remains" of Pan Am Flight #103 in a Lincolnshire scrapyard, 2018. The iconic Pan Am logo is seen as dashes of blue, scattered amongst 375 tons of wreckage.

Visiting my parents' gravesite in 2016 at the Dromavally Burial Grounds, Killorglin. We placed my mother Molly there in 1975, and my father Tom joined her just one year later.

My beautiful, inimitable grandneice Amelia Bambridge 1998–2019

Chapter IV: The Cost of Sorrow

Trauma is a time traveler . . . that reaches back and devours everything that came before.

—Junot Diaz

Darkness returns daily; the sun will always set. Real things do lurk in the shadows because traumatic memories are imprinted on our psyches forever. Regardless of their source, whether from childhood trauma, airline disasters, or an act of terrorism, to name just a few and those I have personal experience with, traumatic events are never fully exorcised. Instead, consciously or unconsciously, we try to banish these memories from being held in the light. We do this for sheer survival, to get out of bed every morning, to continue inhaling and exhaling. But once the immediate shock of the traumatic event dissipates, where do the effects of that trauma go? We may become successful in compartmentalizing it, but it never fully leaves us. In one way or another and by varying degrees, it is deposited directly into the body, where it can manifest as numerous illnesses and all manner of physical and emotional pain. It becomes our constant and most loathed companion.

The world breaks everyone and afterward many are strong at the broken places. But those that will not break it kills. It kills the very good and the very gentle and the very brave impartially. If you are none of these you can be sure it will kill you too but there will be no special hurry.

—Ernest Hemmingway, *A Farewell to Arms*

Just as a fallen apple can never be hung back up on the tree, there is no reversing the impact of trauma. But there is healing to be had. There is, in time, a blunting of the sharp blade of pain, a softening, and a space that opens within us whereby we simply make room for the loss and sadness. This is imperative not only in terms of our own survival but for our long-term physical, mental, and emotional health. Left unexplored, the trauma we've experienced can and will make us sick, and it can kill us. On its journey to that destination, it can sabotage our relationships, ruin our careers, cripple our sense of self-esteem and lay waste to our hopes, dreams, and ambitions. What is not transformed, for example, through therapy, is transmitted to those we love, and the damage can affect our families and loved ones for generations to come.

Traumatic events leave their mark on us all. Sources of trauma are endlessly varied. But if we look exclusively at those caused by domestic terrorism and natural disasters over the last several years, we can usually and immediately remember how we felt when we first heard the news and feel their impact again. The Sandy Hook Elementary School shootings of December 14, 2012, the Orlando nightclub shooting of June 12, 2016, or the Stoneman Douglas High School shooting in Parkland, Florida, on Valentine's Day 2018, come to mind immediately. Natural disasters such as the Indian Ocean earthquake and tsunami of December 26, 2004, Hurricane Katrina on August 23, 2005, or Hurricane Maria, which decimated Dominica and Puerto Rico on September 18–20, 2017, are also fresh visuals for me. Most of us know precisely where we were and what we were doing when those events occurred. These are "flashbulb memories" so powerful that they are permanently tattooed onto our minds. Trauma can and does in fact alter the neural pathways in the brain and cause stress hormones to course through the bloodstream, creating compromised immunities, chronic illness, and disease. Think for a moment about the generational ripple effect of those traumatized by the catastrophic events mentioned above. Imagine growing up as a surviving sibling of a child murdered at

Sandy Hook Elementary or losing your son who was dancing the night away at The Pulse nightclub in Orlando. Imagine being the female child of a woman who was raped, who hasn't trusted a man since, who raises you to likewise distrust any man you encounter. Your fate is not any healthier if you are a male child in that family. That which is not transformed is transmitted. We may personally do everything possible to block our memories of the childhood trauma we experienced, or we may have grown up in a household or community that did the job for us by maintaining a cone of silence on the topic. This is not unusual and is in fact common. Individuals and families suppress the events for many reasons, but in most cases, the reasons get reduced to a toxic brew of guilt and shame, with a potent chaser of blame and defense often paired on the side.

But one way or another, those memories will out. They may surface under certain triggering events, such as the loss of a job, divorce, or a death in the family, or they may be present in a disguised form of anti-social or self-destructive behavior. They may surface during sleep in the form of nightmares. Traumatic memories may also surface with aging. As our lives progress and the daily challenges of child-rearing, career-building, and other keep-busy activities dissipate, we are frequently left with only ourselves and our memories. You may have noticed the elderly are often focused on the past, suggesting that the defenses and distractions of their younger years have fallen away, exposing what has long been buried. There is now a space for these memories to fill, and for the elderly, the future is limited. We come to a time in our lives where, consciously or unconsciously, we begin the process of integration and healing in preparation for our own death, trying to make ourselves whole from our many disparate pieces, perhaps for easier passage.

Vicarious or secondary trauma, caused by terrorism, natural disasters, or an event such as witnessing a violent crime, for example, is in a different category than those traumas experienced in childhood, which are usually repeated over many years. Childhood trauma is not only chronic, but in many cases, it did not originate with that child. This type of trauma is frequently passed down, like a genetic disease, a bad seed. We call this transgenerational or multigenerational trauma. The original trauma is transferred from the first generation of trauma survivors to subsequent generations.

Clinicians first noticed this phenomenon in 1966, when the Canadian children of Holocaust survivors sought psychological treatment in large numbers. A generation later, their children, who were the Holocaust survivors' grandchildren, were referred for treatment 300% more frequently than the general public. The same passing forward of the effects of trauma onto successive generations has been seen in Native American populations whose family elders, as children, were sent away to residential boarding schools, where they were disallowed to speak their native language or practice their native rituals and customs, and where many of them were subjected to emotional, physical, and sexual abuse. Multigenerational trauma has also been seen in the families of combat veterans, prisoners of war, and the families of those victimized by clerical abuse in the church and other religious organizations. It has been seen in the families of victims of domestic and sexual abuse and in families living in abject poverty.[16] It is seen in many of us.

The Adverse Childhood Experiences Study (ACE) conducted in the early 1990s by the HMO Kaiser Permanente in collaboration with the Centers for Disease Control and Prevention (CDC), with on-going long-term monitoring of the participants, has definitively shown a correlation between childhood trauma and life-long health and social problems. Of more than 17,000 people studied, all had jobs and good health care, 75% had attended college, and the average age of the participants was 57 years. These research subjects were asked which of the following types of childhood traumas they had experienced:

- Physical abuse
- Sexual abuse

- Emotional abuse
- Physical neglect
- Emotional neglect
- Exposure to domestic violence
- Household substance abuse
- Household mental illness
- Parental separation or divorce
- Incarcerated household member

The findings showed a strong relationship to health, social and behavioral problems, and substance abuse across the lifespan of the subjects. Nearly a third had experienced physical abuse, and more than 20% had experienced sexual abuse. The researchers also discovered that these ACE/childhood trauma types were often clustered together, with many occurring at the same time. The greater the number of ACE types, the more likely it was that the individual became a smoker, abused alcohol and drugs, was promiscuous, and over time, became severely obese. The greater number of ACE types was also found to correlate with depression, heart disease, cancer, chronic lung disease and a shortened lifespan. Compared to an ACE score of zero, having four adverse childhood experiences was associated with twice the rate of cancer diagnoses and a four-fold increase in emphysema. And for the most traumatized, those with an ACE score above six, it was found they had 30 times the likelihood of having attempted suicide.[17]

The results of the ACE study suggest that childhood trauma/adverse childhood experiences contribute to serious health problems decades later. While the subjects of the study were of a specific demographic of Americans, these findings apply to trends in other demographics seen across the world.[18]

Cognitive and neuroscience researchers have examined potential reasons why this might be so, and it's been found that childhood trauma can change the way neural pathways develop. Trauma can alter how we think, perceive, and behave. Trauma can also change the biochemistry of the neuroendocrine system, which regulates involuntary responses such as breathing, metabolism, energy utilization, and blood pressure, and by doing so, it might result in accelerating disease, aging, and compromise of the immune system. Researchers have also determined that those effects can cross from mother to child, even in pregnancy, presenting a biological possibility of multigenerational trauma in addition to the environmental contributions.[19]

So, what does all this science mean? In summary, it means that if we're not actively engaged in confronting our traumatic memories or working on excavating repressed childhood memories to arrive at an understanding of what we've experienced, trauma will control our lives before possibly bringing that life to a premature ending. Nature and nurture are working in tandem to create a very rough road for those of us who have experienced adverse, not to mention devastating, childhoods. If we don't connect the dots of where we came from and why we act the way we do, and if we don't take active steps to understand all that, then our lives and those of the people we love may likely be chaotic, self-destructive, and marred by illness. Trauma can cause havoc on the mind, body, and spirit. We need to understand this so that we stop asking ourselves and others "What the hell is wrong with you?" and start asking the deeper, kinder question of "What happened?" Because the chances are great that something did.

The ACE studies also showed a definitive correlation between childhood trauma and addiction. Having four or more adverse childhood experiences was associated with an enormous increase in alcoholism over those whose ACE score was zero. My score of five makes me a whopping 700% more likely than not to collect sobriety coins and not keep a corkscrew or martini shaker in the house.

I am a classic example of that ACE study. Of those ten childhood trauma types listed, my score of five was a harbinger. My childhood was shaped by physical and emotional abuse, some degree of neglect, my father's domestic violence and his substance abuse. Five is a bad score. As I read through the findings and associated behaviors, it's as if I'm looking at a blueprint of my own life. I'm an alcoholic, gratefully in recovery for over forty years now. I was promiscuous, which was quite paradoxical to my religious upbringing. That upbringing had always been and continues to be my moral compass regardless of how lost I was in my partying days. As much as I'd like to think that my behavior was a by-product of the time and the place, being a flight attendant in the late 60s and 70s, I must take ownership for the decisions I made in those years; nobody forced me into bed. My ACE score correlates with the possibility of early teenage sexual experience, and this was true in my case. However, the corollary of smoking and my ACE scores do not match up; I was never a smoker. But I did suffer from depression and fibromyalgia, which is now thought to be a consequence of multiple ACE scores. I had suicidal ideation during my drinking period, and I believe it was only my Catholic upbringing that protected me from following through. And I have heart disease, which likely would have killed me had I not undergone surgery in the last few years.

I was a captive of those experiences for the first thirty years of my life. It is only through a lot of personal work, going back to school to gain a deeper understanding of psychology, attending therapy, seeking spiritual connection, and exploring a variety of different therapeutic modalities over these last decades, that I'm no longer held captive. But to move from captive to captain of my own life is an endless discipline, a job with no vacation or sick days allowed, ever.

As a psychologist, I've had the clinical experience of treating patients with addiction and over-reactive, aggressive behaviors whose parents and grandparents suffered addictions and those behaviors as well. These previous generations never transformed their own issues, and so they transmitted them intact to the next generation. Another clinically familiar scenario is treating the patient who personally doesn't drink because her parents and grandparents were alcoholics, but she suffers from dysfunctional thinking, distorted beliefs, and unhealthy behaviors. One needn't have alcohol or substance abuse issues personally to suffer the long-term consequences of having grown up in a family ravaged by addictions or hollowed out by trauma. Trauma does not necessarily cause addiction, and addiction does not automatically cause trauma. But they frequently co-occur, they often contribute to one another, and one can be hidden inside the other like nested Russian dolls.

The status quo in clinical treatment has been treating the addicted as a victim of a genetic disorder and treating the behaviors, seen as the symptoms of the disorder, that manifest in substance abuse. The end goal of treatment has been to create in the patient an impregnable defense against ever having another drink or using again. It's an honorable goal and offers the afflicted and their loved ones a sense of safety, redemption, and respect. As one who has worked in the field of alcohol and drug abuse for more than thirty years, I have employed the tactics and seen sustainable success in many. I've watched broken families heal and been witness to lives on the edge finding and keeping solid ground beneath their feet.

Genetic proclivities are real and inescapable. As a practitioner, I've often seen one child in a family suffer the fate of addiction while her sibling, partaking in a similar degree of substance use, can easily manage without ill effect. But why? What else other than one's genetic makeup accounts for these differences and the differences between those who defeat their addictions and those who don't? What makes one person resilient while another is not? Those of us who have specialized in the treatment of addictions have wrested much of our counseling on the nature/genetics side of this equation. But that's only half the picture. Some are simply more resilient than others. And some have traumatic experiences no one else knows about, which makes them more vulnerable. No two individuals ever respond to the same traumatic experiences in the same way, but understanding the relationship between trauma and addiction is critical to the successful treatment of those who suffer.

Most people admitted for addiction treatment have experienced trauma. The numbers behind this statement are staggering: 80–90% of women who have been sexually abused become addicted. Approximately 50% of people with histories of addiction have experienced trauma. The connection between trauma and addiction is a two-way street: trauma increases the risk of developing addiction, and active addiction increases the likelihood of experiencing trauma. Alcohol abuse affects 54% of men and 28% of women with PTSD.[20] According to the 1992 Bureau of Justice Statistics, "Substances are also used by trauma perpetrators, whether they are under the influence while committing harm (many violent assaults are committed while intoxicated) or whether they use a substance to sedate the victim." Community-wide traumatic disasters, such as terrorist attacks, natural disasters, and mass murders, are also known to lead to widespread increased substance use within that community.[21]

In counseling patients to follow the traditional-oriented philosophy, to stop drinking or using, to go to meetings and to use the well-worn steps, we lead them to the singular goal of having and maintaining a stable foundation. But for patients who have suffered trauma, that foundation is built on sand. When trauma is involved, that advice is nowhere near enough and nowhere near sustainable. For the traumatized, alcohol and other drug use can become a survival strategy, a way to help numb the distress, anxiety, depression, and fear precipitated by trauma. In counseling these patients to abstain, we may unintentionally be stripping them of the very survival techniques their lives, in whole or in part, depend on to function. Suppressed trauma breaks through when the anesthetic of using ends, and untreated trauma can lead to relapse.

I had denied my traumatic childhood experiences for so long and then denied my own drunken adult behaviors. For many years I was able to compartmentalize these experiences; I intellectualized and dismissed them because of my job and the freewheeling times I came of age in. But when I stopped drinking, the childhood memories broke through, flooding me with shame, guilt and their by-product, depression. At the time, I was living in NYC and was lucky to find a superb therapist who specialized in addiction and, perhaps more importantly, its consequences. My therapist placed me on the road to healing, a path I've never stepped away from.

I think it's imperative that we provide compassion and comfort to patients by understanding that their behavior may be a metaphor for unresolved trauma. They may likely be acting out traumatic history without knowing that it leads to self-destructive behaviors. The patient may not have a language to describe what specifically she was subjected to, or she may have no memory of it at all. In order to begin a healing process, that story must be gently brought to the surface and told.

People have a hard time letting go of their suffering. Out of a fear of the unknown, they prefer suffering that is familiar.[22]

Personally, I do believe addiction in and of itself is a primary illness that is chronic, progressive, and potentially fatal. Even so, I have come to understand that individuals treated for alcoholism and other substance abuse need to be evaluated for their experiences of traumatic events. As a psychologist, I think it's essential that a trauma history be taken in the early stages of treatment, as unacknowledged trauma can lead the patient to be non-compliant with medical advice, to repeat self-defeating behaviors, and to use again.

I served as vice president of treatment services for seven years at the Betty Ford Center in Rancho Mirage, California. The Center was started in 1982 by the wife of the thirty-eighth US President, Gerald Ford; she courageously sought treatment for her own addictions to alcohol and prescription drugs. Her lofty and very public profile as First Lady moved the subject of addictions into the national spotlight and brought hope of recovery to many, especially women.

One of my major contributions to the Betty Ford Center was to bring a body of trauma-oriented treatment methodologies into our treatment plan. I do believe that the Center was one of the first in the country to incorporate a trauma history survey as part of the patient's intake process, allowing the nurses and physicians to be sensitive and mindful in planning the patient's treatment. It had been my hope, and I lectured exhaustively on the subject, that the use of the trauma survey would become standard practice in the field of recovery, given the high percentage in the general population of those suffering addictions having also experienced trauma.

One day after a lecture I'd given, a patient, a very successful physician who had been in the audience, approached me. I'd just been speaking about the correlation between trauma and addiction, and he told me that my subject matter had allowed him, in an "aha moment," to identify the cause of his own relapse after twenty years of positive recovery. He had so deeply buried his childhood experience of being sexually abused that he hadn't shared it with anyone, including his therapist and sponsor. Because his trauma had never been disclosed, he felt it had eventually hijacked his recovery. Identifying this correlation between his repressed childhood experience and his relapse was, he went on to say, not only liberating but also empowering. We have stayed in touch over the years; we speak every year on the annual anniversary of his recovery. He has not had a relapse since. His understanding of and giving voice to his childhood abuse allowed him to end his own cycle of using that trauma as an unconscious organizing principle around which he'd built his life. His understanding freed him.

But many years later, trauma history surveys still have not become standard practice in the field. In an article written by John Lavitt and published on January 6, 2016, in the Fix, a website for alcohol and drug addiction recovery news and information, Dr. Gabor Maté is interviewed in an article titled "Addiction is a Response to Childhood Suffering." A

Hungarian-born Canadian physician with a specialty in childhood trauma and the correlation to lifelong physical, emotional and mental health, Dr. Maté said the following:

> 'A recent article in *the New York Times* revealed how it's now been shown that the life expectancy of middle-class whites is going down. More and more are dying before their time, and ... much of that decrease in longevity is being caused by drug overdoses, and the effects of drug and alcohol use on this population ... However, nobody's linking that to trauma ... Dr. Oz will have a show on addiction ... but trauma won't be mentioned. Society and the medical profession are in denial of the role of trauma in this problem. If we are in denial of trauma, we're never going to understand addiction ... We just keep talking about this bad problem of addiction, but we don't want to look at what it's really all about.'

As a professional in the field of recovery for more than thirty years, I believe that's right.

While I haven't been directly involved in working in an inpatient treatment center since resigning as CEO of the Las Vegas Recovery Center in 2016, I continue to consult with individuals and treatment facilities. I'm watching with great interest the changing trends in psychopharmacology and the use of non-pharmacological therapies in treating addictions, depression, and other psychological consequences of trauma.

Some of the therapies being introduced as new are actually recycled, "new again," a return to usage that was restricted or shut down completely in the 1960s when some of these natural psychotropics were taken out of the laboratories and used for recreational use in the streets. We're now seeing a revival of a field that began in 1943 when LSD was found to be an effective panacea for migraines.

Throughout the 1950s and '60s, psychedelic experiments were conducted in university and lab settings involving tens of thousands of patients. Regarded by scientists at the time as a legitimate area of inquiry, the research was pursued in relation to a wide range of mental processes and disorders, including autism, schizophrenia, and the existential distress associated with a terminal illness and pending death. In those years, the most extensively studied subject was the treatment for alcoholism, although the results were ambiguous at best in terms of an effective and lasting treatment for the alcoholic.[23]

But some of those findings did show an interesting, non-direct correlation. A newfound sense of spirituality is linked to the use of psychedelics, and spirituality has been linked to the study of alcohol addiction since at least the late nineteenth century when the philosopher and psychologist William James observed alcoholics attaining sobriety after what he termed "conversions." In *The Varieties of Religious Experience* published in 1902, James described alcoholics who, often in concert with fasting or intense prayer, felt a "divine presence" that radically changed them and mitigated their cravings for the bottle.

A significant "conversion" occurred to a gentleman by the name of Bill Wilson, who happened to be the co-founder of Alcoholics Anonymous (A.A.). Wilson had been a feckless drunk whose repeated attempts to get sober failed miserably. At a Manhattan clinic frequented by the sodden and well-heeled, doctors administered a treatment they called the "belladonna cure." Belladonna is a plant in the nightshade family, known since the Middle Ages for causing hallucinations and delirium. According to his writings, Wilson witnessed a "blinding white light shining" through his hospital window and felt "caught up into an ecstasy which there are no words to describe. A great peace stole over me, and I thought, no matter how wrong things seem to be, they are still all right." He coined this experience the "essential All-Rightness of the universe," and it ultimately led to his life-long sobriety. He structured A.A. based on principles of honesty, accountability, social support, and acceptance of a higher power, which summarized the epiphany he had had under the influence of the belladonna.

Wilson also used LSD. He was a friend of Aldous Huxley, the English novelist who wrote *Brave New World* and nearly fifty other books. Huxley was prominent among a group of artists, intellectuals, and psychologists experimenting with LSD. In a letter to the Catholic theologian Thomas Merton, Huxley wrote that Wilson had compared the experience to the "spontaneous theophany which changed his life as completely as St. Paul's was changed on the road to Damascus." Theophany is the visible manifestation of God, or a god, to mankind.

Regardless of what initiated Bill Wilson's spiritual experience and recovery from alcoholism, he charted new territory that has led to sobriety for millions. A.A. boasts over two million members in 180 nations, with more than 118,000 groups. In 1999, twenty-eight years after his death, *Time Magazine* listed Bill Wilson as one of the 100 most important people of the century.

And yet, for many years, medical researchers and many psychotherapists were unsure whether Alcoholics Anonymous worked better than other approaches to treating people with alcohol use disorder. But in March of 2020, an extensive analysis was conducted by the Stanford School of Medicine, which gave us a compelling reason to believe in the fellowship's efficacy. The evaluation was comprised of 35 studies involving the work of 135 scientists and more than 10,000 participants, comprised of the young, elderly, male, female, veterans, and civilians, conducted in five different countries.

Dr. Keith Humphreys, professor of psychology and behavioral sciences at Stanford University (and an esteemed advisor to the National Drug Control Policy under Presidents Bush and Obama, and consultant to state and local governments on addiction and public health and safety practices), determined that A.A. was nearly always found to be 60% more effective than psychotherapy or no intervention at all. This is a humbling acknowledgment from a lauded psychologist who, early in his career, once said of A.A., "How dare these people do things that I have all these degrees to do?" But Humphreys is now resolute. "A.A. works because it's based on social interaction," he says, noting that members give one another emotional support as well as practical tips to refrain from drinking. "If you want to change your behavior, find some other people who are trying to make the same change," he said.

The review was published in the *Cochrane Database of Systematic Review*. *Cochrane* is a global independent network of researchers, professionals, patients, and others interested in health. "Cochrane Reviews are the gold standard in medicine for integration of all the research about a particular intervention," Humphreys said. "We wanted to do this work through Cochrane because of its rigor and reputation." While it was beyond the scope of their study, Humphreys said the A.A. review is "certainly suggestive that these methods work for people who use heroin or cocaine . . . It absolutely does work," he said of A.A.'s methodology.

We know that an alcoholic negatively impacts many people; this is not an individual struggle but rather one that affects the family, community, and society at large. Just as the alcoholic may have suffered trauma in the past, his addiction now causes trauma for those around him. Given the impact can be so broad, Dr. Humphreys' conclusions about the importance of social interaction and peer support as a critical feature of therapy make perfect sense to me: those who are hurt can become those who help heal.

Medical doctors and researchers continue to seek new methodologies in the treatment of addictions. A prominent substance abuse researcher at Johns Hopkins named Roland Griffiths published a study in 2006 looking at both the immediate and long-term psychological effects of a high dose of psilocybin delivered to 36 healthy volunteers. The study found that "magic mushrooms" reliably resulted in a "mystical-type" experience that was known by Wilson and Huxley. It is also well-defined in classical scholarship of religion, including a sense of awe, ineffability, and profound awareness of the unity of all things. Griffith's study found that the participants reported positive changes in their mental well-being and behavior for many months afterward. A third of the participants rated the session as the most spiritually significant experience of their lives, and 80 percent rated it among their top five meaningful life experiences ever.

Additionally, in an article titled "Treating Addiction with Psychedelics," published in *Scientific American* on January 1, 2017, current research on the hallucinogen ibogaine has shown promise in treating alcoholism. Some who have tried it in "underground" clinical settings report near instant relief from cravings and withdrawal symptoms. There are promising results from animal studies of new drugs that mimic ibogaine's chemical structure but without the hallucinations. Additional testing in mice and rats has shown reduced self-medication of cocaine, opioids, and nicotine. If further testing shows promising results, addiction treatment as we've known it may change significantly.

These findings, while certainly interesting and hopeful, are preliminary. It's important to remember that these psychoactive drugs are not FDA-approved, and consequently, much of the research is currently coming from other countries, including Canada and Thailand. It's a very long and expensive road from the laboratory to FDA approval, manufacture, and delivery of a new therapy. It's also important to remember that the side effects of some of these compounds can be dangerous. These experiments have all been conducted in a highly controlled environment managed by a psychologist and medical doctor who oversaw the experience and monitored the patient for several days afterward.

My own preference is Medical Assisted Treatment (MAT), which combines behavioral therapy and medications to treat substance use disorders. It too relies on supervision by the prescribing physician, along with psychosocial support. This is a holistic approach in terms of understanding the psychological, social, cultural, and genetic causes of addiction. Addressing each of these components is necessary to achieve a sustainable outcome. MAT is a safe and effective treatment methodology and may include involvement in a program. In my own practice of evaluating and treating patients who suffer from the disease of addiction, I refer them to work in tandem with counselors and physicians who specialize in addictions. There are many well-intended and excellent healthcare providers and a nearly constant influx of new treatment methodologies to explore, but only those specifically trained and certified as addiction specialists can effectively address the complexities and potential co-morbidity issues that are at play for those who suffer addictions.

A.A. is one of many programs, such as fellowships for drug, food, sex, and gambling addictions, and those formed to help support the family members and adult children of each. Their approaches have a common denominator, and that is the assumption that dependencies are a medical disease and indicative of a spiritual deficit. But my own experiences, both personally and professionally, have taught me that dependencies are not just about genetics or a scarcity of faith; they are also about a surplus of trauma. The causal relationship between addictions and trauma is, for me, the relationship between the lock and key. The experiences of my own life and those of my clients have clearly demonstrated the insidious ways unresolved trauma impacts our own lives, the lives of our family members and future generations to come. I've spent the last twenty years of my professional life addressing this in the form of writing, lecturing, and consulting on the topic of healing from multigenerational trauma and addictions. The experienced, intuitive clinician will feel confident in combining therapeutic models or elements of models, and each individual patient will make choices based on their own needs and circumstances. We want treatment models to be used as roadmaps, but there are times when we need to get off the highways and traverse the dirt roads to meet the individual's needs. While I'm not unconditionally condoning the experimentation of any of the plant-based therapies for those who suffer the ravages of addictions or mental health issues, I do think we may be on the brink of a new era in treatment options. I fully support the need to stay open-minded and focused on the goal. That goal is healing for the traumatized alcoholic. That goal is sustainable recovery for the addict. That goal is freeing the mind, body, and spirit of the poisons in the bloodstream, whether infected by our own injurious experiences or those unwittingly passed down to us by our elders. That goal is to leave the shadow world and stand in the light of day, upright, whole, proud, and safe at last.

Chapter V: A Map of the Self

Animae mundi colendae gratia: for the sake of tending soul in and of the world.
—Motto of Pacifica Graduate Institute

Nestled between the Pacific Ocean and the Santa Ynez Mountain range, built on a coastal plain, the small city of Carpinteria, California, rests in the shade of the tallest Torrey pine tree in the world. Just east of Santa Barbara, the city was named "the carpentry shop" in 1769 by the explorers of the Spanish Portola expedition after seeing several Chumash villagers building a canoe there. If your car windows are rolled down, you can hear the seals and sea lions barking as you drive to the beach, known for its gentle slope and serene waves, while in other spots, surfers will find respectable swells crashing against the rock jetties.

There is something holy about this place, something that has been calling me to it for more than thirty years now. I was attending an annual summer conference there, at Pacifica Graduate Institute, on July 18, 1996, when I received the call that TWA Flight #800 had exploded over Long Island Sound. I have returned to Carpinteria regularly. While not logical, there's something about the geography that reminds me of my birth home in Killorglin, Ireland. Maybe it's the fog that snakes above the surface of the ground, or the nearness of the mountains, and that magical juxtaposition of solid high ground and low-lying bodies of water. Maybe it's the commonality of the pine and oak trees, or specifically that enormous Torrey pine, standing like a 126-foot sentry downtown, reminding me of the tall metal cross standing guard at the top of Mount Brandon. Perhaps it's all the above or none, something else altogether. But like a river pushed to the sea, I feel a forceful pull and deep connection to Carpinteria. I sought something there, and I return to that source regularly.

Some places exist on hallowed ground. Native American burial grounds and other areas where a great number of lives were lost, such as the site of the World Trade Center in New York or Omaha Beach in Normandy, just to mention a few. Many of these places have astonishing natural beauty, remarkable architecture or powerful works of art. Some may just feel imbued with a sense of spirituality. I have felt it in numerous places, such as Santa Fe, New Mexico, and Assisi, Italy. Certainly, those grounds that for centuries have been the routes of pilgrimages, like the Camino de Santiago in Spain, Camino Francés in France, the pilgrimage to the Temple in Jerusalem, or the area marked by the crosses on Mount Brandon, are all steeped in a feeling of grace and gravitas.

Going to Carpinteria was, at first unconsciously, my own pilgrimage. I was seeking understanding and insight to salve existential angst. I was seeking a spiritual life, a calling I'd had as a youngster when I imagined becoming a nun, which had gotten swept sideways in the living of my life. I was seeking healing, but from what, I wasn't quite sure. And I was seeking a sense of reciprocity and balance, but I didn't know what that really meant. We live our lives walking forward, but we learn about ourselves only by looking back. I was pulled to Carpinteria to attend Pacifica Graduate Institute, but only after completing the arduous labor of writing my thesis there did I realize why. "The conflict between the will to deny horrible events and the will to proclaim them aloud is the central dialectic of psychological trauma."[24]

Pacifica Graduate Institute, where I earned my doctorate of philosophy in clinical psychology in 2004, was founded in the early 1970s to provide mental health services to the local community. A dozen years later, a masters level program was created in Counseling Psychology with an emphasis in "depth psychology," followed shortly thereafter by a doctorate program. Course work included in-depth studies of Sigmund Freud, Carl Jung, alchemy, Hippocratic medicine, dream interpretation, mythology, and classical literature. Joseph Campbell, the author and mythologist, was an early supporter of the Institute, which now holds his collection of three thousand books.

Depth psychology is defined as "the study of unconscious mental processes and motives, especially in psychoanalytic theory and practice." It is based on the thinking that some thoughts, emotions, wishes, and memories are accessible (conscious), while others exist but are not accessible (unconscious). Freud, Jung, and others worked with their patients to illuminate the unconscious and integrate those feelings and memories into the conscious mind to make whole an individual who, perhaps through trauma, repression, or addiction, was bifurcated, rent in two.

Depth psychology is considered the psychology of the psyche/soul and claims to furnish a key to exploring the unconscious mind. Broadly speaking, depth psychology operates according to the following assumptions: The psyche is a process, a verb rather than a noun, which is partly conscious and partly unconscious. The unconscious contains repressed experiences and other personal issues in its "upper," close-to-the-surface layers and "transpersonal" (e.g., collective, archetypal) forces deeper down.

The psyche spontaneously generates mythical-religious symbolism and is, therefore, spiritual as well as instinctive in nature. Perhaps the value of a depth psychological approach is not how much we know or learn about the unconscious but rather coming to understand that the unconscious holds knowledge about us that, when revealed, can help us lead happier and healthier lives. Put another way, it's the difference between gaining knowledge and the application of that knowledge.

Dr. Stephen Aizenstat, therapist and founding president and chancellor at Pacifica, explains,

> 'Through the study of dreams, images, symptoms, slips of the tongue, spontaneous humor, meaningful coincidences as well as interpersonal engagements, depth psychologists attempt to understand the language and the dynamics of the unconscious as it manifests in their work with clients and in the world. Depth psychological approaches to psychological suffering attempt to help individuals become aware of what has been cast out of consciousness or not yet able to be known. Healing is associated with allowing what has been repressed, rejected, denied, or ignored to come forward so that the person can understand, explore its significance, and integrate it, allowing for a transformation in consciousness. Depth Psychology also attends to the way unconscious processes express themselves in society and culture, and how culture affects the psyche.'

As an example of the unconscious expressing itself in my life, the night of the Lockerbie disaster, I dreamt that my close friend, Gerry Murphy, was on board Pan Am Flight #103. When I woke up and thought about this dream, I suddenly had a visceral response: my body shook, and my heart leapt. I thought little of this until an hour later when I went to my office in Pan Am's medical department at JFK airport and was handed the crew list. My friend Mary Geraldine (Gerry) Murphy's name stood out in stark relief. My knees nearly buckled.

Another example of this occurred while walking on the beach in Carpinteria. It was 5:30 p.m. on July 17, 1996. My calm was suddenly punctured by what felt like a sudden punch to the solar plexus; I immediately felt ill and disoriented. As soon as I got to my car to return to the hotel, my beeper went off to call TWA operations: Flight #800 had just disappeared from the radar.

I have no doubt in my mind that I'd connected with my friend, Gerry Murphy, and with the souls who perished on TWA Flight #800 through our collective unconscious, a concept Jung introduced to explain a form of the unconscious mind common to all mankind. Dreams and sudden sensations like these were common for me. Since early childhood, I've had these kinds of experiences and innate psychic, intuitive abilities. I grew to honor them as a gift from God and my Celtic roots: Ireland is steeped in mythology and the belief in the unknown, populated by ghosts, fairies, and spirit guides communicating to us. Our unconscious mind knows before our conscious mind is aware. It is easy to dismiss these events or to sweep them under the coincidence rug. But my training in depth psychology, along with understanding my Celtic heredity, taught me to access the organic, universal knowledge we all have as animals and to allow that knowledge and those senses to inform me. For several years, I had been in and out of analysis in St. Louis. My analyst, who had been trained at the Jungian Institute in Zurich, brought to my attention the importance of the collective unconscious, dreams, and mythology. I began to research doctoral programs and found Pacifica Graduate Institute, where I began my advanced studies in the fall of 2000. I knew I wanted to write my dissertation on the vicarious traumatization of airline employees in the aftermath of an airline disaster.

But a year later, I thought my research would be insignificant, perhaps even redundant, in the wake of a large body of published findings flooding the mental health field following the events of September 11, 2001. I seriously considered abandoning the topic, but ultimately, I was encouraged to stick with it, in an ironic twist, by the crewmembers I'd been interviewing for my research; my subjects convinced me of the importance of my own research. The flight attendants shared that they had felt abandoned and overlooked, considering all the other fatalities on 9/11. They repeatedly expressed a need to be seen, recognized, and validated for the trauma they themselves had endured, and they desperately wanted to honor their fellow fallen crewmembers, those who'd been murdered on the four planes that went down that day. This sense of reciprocity and balance, of helping others to heal while doing my own work, which in large part was driven by my need to heal myself, was an astounding moment of awakening for me. It was an epiphany.

> *The final stage of healing is to help others to heal . . . Move from victim to survivor to activist/advocate for change.*[25]

It was just the first of many revelations I would experience at Pacifica that, looking back, I see placed me firmly on a spiritual path that has guided my life, my relationships, and my work over these last two decades. As a child, I'd wanted to become a nun; what I was learning here is that one needn't wear a habit and live in a convent to be in the service of others under the guidance of a greater whole. "Run to the rescue and peace will follow," said the late River Phoenix, the multi-talented performer and animal activist, at the young age of seventeen. He'd had no formal education, and here I was, nearly twice that age and with multiple degrees, and only now getting it.

As I became more engrossed in my studies, I began to see the imagery and symbolism of my Catholic upbringing through a more psychological, less religious lens. The iconography of the church became less literal and more symbolic to me. For example, paintings of the Mother Mary holding the infant Jesus now represents to me Mother Earth holding the planet and all its beautiful, sentient beings. The deeper I got into depth psychology, the more sense my world, and all its superficially divergent aspects, suddenly made. What had been stand-alone facts, a painfully shy Irish girl growing up in poverty and in a violent household, who became an alcoholic while being a glamorous airline stewardess, who pursued advanced degrees in an obscure niche of psychology, who then became an executive at an internationally-renowned drug and alcohol rehab center before returning to the work of grief counseling and training in the wake of community-wide tragedies and terrorist attacks, all these head-scratching and disparate markers of my life began to coalesce. My life was a gestalt, the whole of it larger than the sum of all these parts. There are times in my work as a clinician when I search to find a metaphor that best describes what transpires between my client and me. The metaphor of being a "spiritual midwife" resonates with me. Essentially, what happens over the course of our treatment together is I assist the client in bringing forth their latent inner strengths and natural born gifts. A midwife is one who helps deliver a new life. I like to believe I help my clients deliver new self-awareness, which can lead them to live new lives.

Traditional psychoanalysis is a voyage of self-discovery with the goal of healing psychic wounds, helping people grow emotionally, maximizing their potential, and becoming enlivened by a renewed sense of their individual path in life. Addiction recovery calls for the care of the soul, and this requires of the patient a willingness to learn themselves and to allow the caregiver access to that process. As a caregiver, I acknowledge that experiencing the emotions of grief and witnessing the pain, sadness, and difficulties of others on a regular basis reaches down into my own reservoirs of unresolved grief and pain. As a psychotherapist, I strive to continue my own journey of rigorous self-examination, to realize the joy and pain of "knowing oneself." I believe a psychologist cannot take a patient any further than they themselves have gone or are willing to go. Really knowing and understanding how a traumatized, recovering individual feels is best achieved by knowing oneself.

Whatever the reasons had been that led me to Carpinteria, I had enough awareness to follow the calling. I was now gaining insight, clarity, and purpose, and I now had faith in myself and in my part in the greater good. And perhaps most importantly, I had begun to exorcise the various traumatic events from my childhood and young adulthood. Having been unaware that I'd been repressing those memories for all those years, I was stunned by the force of their hold and the depth of their roots. It takes the young child years to understand that the flower she sees in the garden isn't the whole plant, that it's merely an aboveground extension of a complex system she can't see, a system that actually is the cause and manager of that flower. All those delicate hair-like roots create a multi-purpose structure for water and nutrient absorption, to anchor and support the flower, to store food and mineral supplies, to support reproduction. At Pacifica, I was only now beginning to understand the complex system of my own subterranean environment that produced the woman I called "myself." This was a kind of revelation, a kind of enlightenment. It set me on a path I've been on since, without waver or wane.

How could I, or anyone, turn away from the sense of liberation that knowledge and understanding can give us? It was my immersion into depth psychology that was molding order out of the chaos within me. I felt what I think A.A. founder Bill Wilson had referred to as the "essential All-Rightness of the universe." I felt what the researcher Roland Griffith of Johns Hopkins had reported his research subjects feeling: a "mystical-type experience . . . like those defined in classical scholarship of religion, including a sense of awe, ineffability, and profound awareness of the unity of all things."

Chapter VI: Transformation and Transcendence

The most effective way to destroy people is to deny and obliterate their own understanding of their history.
—George Orwell

One of the most profound and transformative experiences I've had in my life was in 2007. I and a group of volunteer counselors from the Betty Ford Clinic, where I was then serving as vice president of treatment services, spent a week with the Alkali Lake people, an indigenous tribal community of four hundred in Northern British Columbia. Their story is told in a 1986 film titled *The Honour of All: The Story of Alkali Lake*.

We travelled to their community on the Shuswap Indian Reserve as members of a professional team involved in helping the community cope with multigenerational trauma caused by the transmission of alcoholism and sexual abuse. From the depths of addiction, depression, PTSD, and social devastation, the Alkali Lake people were desperately seeking a dramatic change, but by following what was, to me, an unusual and even risky process. What I witnessed there was unlike anything I'd experienced in my clinical practice before.

A combination of events had led to the conditions that afflicted this community, including the systematic removal, in the late nineteenth and early twentieth centuries, of children off the reservation. They were sent to government-run boarding schools, known as "Indian Residential Schools," whose mission was to "civilize" and "Christianize" the children in accordance with European-American standards. This "education" was defined by disallowing the children to speak their native language and practice their native customs. Their long, glossy hair was cut, and their birth names were changed. Across the country, young people were being torn from their parents, family, and cultural life. It was later learned that as part of this assault on native culture, the children were subjected to pervasive physical, emotional, and sexual abuse while attending these schools, resulting not only in the trauma of an entire generation but intentional, systematic decimation of identity and self-worth. By the mid-1980s, upward of 90 percent of the entire population of Alkali Lake young people had been sexually abused.

When the children were returned to their villages, most had no way or wherewithal to understand what had happened to them. And so unwittingly, as the years went by, the self-destructive coping and masking mechanisms of alcoholism, violence, and abuse were passed forward to successive generations.

What the Alkali Lake people wanted was a process promoting healing, which they defined as the restoration of balance, not a process driven by a desire to punish. As they saw it, their need was to interrupt the cycle of abuse so that healthy relationships could be restored. This culturally rooted philosophy eventually led to the development of a very different kind of approach to reconciliation, with a broad network of support and involvement of the chief, tribal council, a core group of volunteers, the local justice system, community workshops, A.A. meetings, psychologists, and traditional, native forms of spirituality and healing. Essentially, a model community was put together, a small community within a larger community, allowing for healing from the inside out.

From my perspective, one of the most astounding strategies used to accomplish this was participation in a survivors and abusers support group, in which the abusers faced their victim(s) and the victims' families, as well as their own family members. To say this process was painful and extremely uncomfortable for everyone participating would be a gross understatement. All the other volunteer clinicians and I had been classically trained in Anglo-American psychology; our methodologies conflicted with what we were asked to facilitate at the Alkali Lake community. Our group discussed the potential risks of having perpetrators and survivors together in the same room, but after input from the tribal chief and elders, we decided to give this format a try.

When the victims/survivors gradually began to feel comfortable or at least supported in the environment, they began to give words to the abuse that they had numbed by alcohol. A tidal wave of repressed trauma emerged, pitting victims (mostly women) against their perpetrators (mostly men), whose first response, predictably, was anger and denial. I sat mesmerized as I watched one of the Alkali Lake women confidently stand in front of her abuser and say loudly, for all to hear, "YOU violated me. YOU sexually abused me!" She wasn't in tears, and she wasn't intimidated; she was presenting a fact. She had rung a bell that could not be un-rung, and at that moment, I witnessed the cloak of her victimhood suddenly slipping from her shoulders. Our eyes now on him, her abuser had to face her as he absorbed her words; he calmly listened before acknowledging that he had done awful things when he was under the influence of alcohol. He was in substance abuse recovery now and was finally able to find the words they both needed to hear. "I'm sorry. I'm so sorry." This was not the end; it was the beginning of healing for this woman and this man and for their community.

Up to that moment, it had been my team's experience that victims usually avoided the perpetrator to every extent possible. We do anything we can to turn away from the memories linked to our trauma; we try to avoid the people, places, and events associated with those experiences. But when trauma is perpetrated within a tight-knit community, especially one relatively isolated, such as those living on Native American lands, it's not possible for victims to avoid their perpetrators. Those who are traumatized are likely to see and regularly interact with the person who violated them. Sometimes they're sitting across the breakfast room table from them.

For the Alkali Lake women, there had been no hiding place, no safe haven. And yet here they were, standing straight, looking directly into the eyes of their tormentors, and calling it for exactly what it was. The impact this had on me cannot be measured. At that moment, I learned that the perpetrator and the survivor could be healed in a shared space instead of perpetuating the familiar method of separating each to protect them both. And a lot of what I knew as a woman, in terms of what would keep *me* safe and what *I* had a *right* to say and do, was likewise transformed at that moment. The power and strength demonstrated by these women astounded me. They did not see themselves as victims; instead, they began to emerge as magnificent, emboldened survivors.

The other psychologists and I had gone there to be of help, support, and assistance, and yet it was we who were enriched. The very thing I feared, and most of my trauma clients had feared, was shown to be the very thing that could set us free. Confronting the enemy and going face-to-face with the one who abused us did not usher in further trauma or otherwise place us back into harm's way. It could break the cycle and transfer the perceived power from other to self. It could flip the paradigm. I'm not suggesting this approach be used universally, but where one is constantly exposed to both perpetrator and survivor, and where both sides are seeking healing, this approach can be life-changing.

This experience was a fundamental building block in my understanding of the relationship between addiction and trauma, and I began to see the two as conjoined twins: each with a heartbeat and central nervous system of its own, and yet integrally merged.

Forgiveness is giving up the hope that the past could have been any different. [26]

As I'd learned from the Alkali Lake women, an essential skill in recovery is to help shift the patient's mindset from that of "victim" to "survivor." Victims are relatively helpless, tossed about by external sources like fallen leaves in the wind. Survivors, on the other hand, are deeply rooted. They become the tree itself and may sway and bend, but they don't topple or break. Survivors grow empowered through the utilization of their internal strengths and resources and frequently, as was the case for the Alkali Lake women, with the support of their communities and peers. With time and care, they transform their experience and their self-perception, which in turn allows them to contain the damage so that it is not transmitted down the line.

While the story of the Alkali Lake community was told in the movie *The Honour of All* thirty-two years ago, a recent broadcast on NPR, titled "The Conflicting Educations of Sam Schimmel,"[27] underscored the long shelf life of community-wide, transgenerational trauma. In Sam's case, a different strategy than that used by the Alkali Lake people was described, with what appears to be a highly effective outcome preventing the third generation from suffering the consequences of unresolved trauma that most certainly damaged the previous two.

"The Conflicting Educations of Sam Schimmel" describes an approach to resolving multigenerational trauma among, again, a Native American population that hinges on immersion in the native culture. Perhaps the research to support this conclusion wasn't yet in when I visited the Alkali Lake village, but certainly, that community was instinctively onto something thirty years ago that science has since supported. The NPR segment tells the story of a Native American boy, Sam, now a young adult, who has been raised both in Alaska and Washington State. Like a generation of Alkali Lake children, Sam's grandmother was removed from her village in Gambell, Alaska, on the shores of the Bering Sea on St. Lawrence Island when she was in middle school. Enforced by the Department of the Interior, the boarding school she was sent to was 1,200 miles away. Most of the teachers were white; English was the only language spoken, and the mission was brutal in its simplicity: cultural annihilation. The program, started by Army officer Richard Pratt in 1879, was first introduced as the Carlisle Indian Industrial School in Pennsylvania before rolling out nationally. Pratt's intention behind his compulsory education model was not limited to the Native American population; his special form of racism knew no discriminatory boundaries and was applied to African Americans, Puerto Ricans, Mexicans and Latinos, Asian Americans, and those with different religious beliefs, such as the Mormons. In 1892, he was quoted as saying, "A great general has said that the only good Indian is a dead one. In a sense, I agree with the sentiment, but only in this: that all the Indian there is in the race should be dead. Kill the Indian in him, and save the man."

Sam's grandmother was stripped of her identity, cultural roots, and traditions, and she experienced the same emotional, physical, and sexual abuse as the Alkali Lake people—and thousands of others—had as well. Sam's mother grew up in a household where her mother's unresolved trauma crossed over to her, and while Sam's mother matured to be an accomplished, highly educated professional woman, she carried and eventually manifested the consequences of her mother's repressed trauma. She suffered from depression, suicidal thoughts, and drug and alcohol abuse. Because she herself was raised in a household of alcoholism, harsh treatment, and emotional remoteness, she didn't have the skills to raise Sam differently.

> ". . . A family goes through something cataclysmic—in this case, a war on their culture. The family survives, but the effects of the trauma are passed down in the form of addiction, domestic violence and even suicide."[28]

What Sam's mother and grandmother suffered ran rampant through their village of Gambell. But the devastating effects on the family and community seem to have been arrested for young Sam. His parents both felt it was important to raise him within the cultural norms of his heritage. As a little boy, he spent a lot of time with his great grandmother and other elders who taught him the "old ways" of fishing, hunting and being at home in the natural world. They filled the child's head and heart with traditional songs and stories. He had a foot in two worlds: his life in Seattle, where his mother had a professional career, and in Alaska, where his father ran a wilderness guiding business. During the summers and holidays, he was an eager, precocious, and unquenchably curious member of a traditional community that had lived on the shores of the Bering Sea for thousands of years. Where his school peers in Seattle were immersed in video games, television, and soccer, he was becoming a state champion sharpshooter with additional passions in hunting and fishing. Sam says,

> "I see that, among my peers, I am much less likely to fall prey to alcoholism and much less likely to be suicidal as a result of being brought up in the laps of my elders, listening to stories and being engaged on a cultural level . . . when youth are not culturally engaged, you see higher rates of incarceration, higher rates of suicide, higher rates of alcoholism, higher rates of drug abuse—all these evils that come in and take the place of culture . . ."

While the entire story of young Sam won't be known for many years, he believes his sense of purpose and sense of self, both unusual in a nineteen-year-old, springs from the integration of his traditional culture into his post-millennial, "Gen Z" life. If the programmatic evisceration of a people's culture results in trauma and its devastating byproducts, wouldn't it follow that healing would be realized in a subsequent generation steeped in and nurtured by its native culture?

Another example of multigenerational, cultural trauma—one that is rooted in my very DNA—is the story of the "hedge schools" in Ireland. The schools were implemented by ordinary Irish Catholic parents to provide rudimentary education to their children; these kids would otherwise be deprived of state-sanctioned education under British law. While the name suggests that classes were held outside, with the students and teachers hiding under the cover of a hedgerow, classes were held in private homes or outbuildings. By the mid 1820s, some 400,000 Irish children were educated this way, in secrecy, in violation of the government, as innocents persecuted for the religious beliefs of their parents. Consequently, the children, their parents and teachers were perceived as defiant, even criminal.

While all Catholic schools were forbidden under British law from 1723 to 1782 in an effort to "anglicize" the middle class: "Want your children educated? Then you must convert to Anglicanism," no hedge teachers or parents were known to have been prosecuted. Formal schools for Catholic under-trained teachers began to appear after 1800, and by the 1830s, the hedge schools were in decline with the implementation of the National School system. But while their numbers were in decline, the hedge schools still existed into the 1890s, suggesting they existed as much from rural poverty and a lack of resources as from religious oppression. My mother's insistence that her children pursue education, I believe, was born out of the cultural trauma and secretive existence of the hedge schools, coupled with the country's history of famine, civil war, and persecution. Of the six children, I am the only one who pursued graduate studies, but all my siblings grew to be successful citizens of the world. My mother did not want to perpetuate the trauma of poverty and brutality that defined her own life; she did not want to transmit the pain down the line.

The trauma caused by community-wide violence ripples through society like a rock thrown into a lake. Where the Alkali Lake community, Sam Schimmel, and my own mother's trauma from cultural repression and abuse was imprinted on our respective lives, I now see nationwide trauma in this country as a direct result of addiction, especially to opioids and alcohol, always alcohol, and gun violence. The worst acts of domestic terrorism in this country have resulted in a body of research tracing the effects on survivors, family members, healthcare workers, and the community at large. In the aftermath of these events, common traits emerge and unite us all in a membership no one would ever choose to join.

Ninety percent of those directly exposed to mass shootings can suffer post-traumatic stress disorder, [29] and experts say that typically up to 40% of survivors, including people who were injured during the assault, their relatives and close friends, experience vicarious or secondary PTSD, according to Leo Flanagan, Jr., a psychologist with Tuesday's Children, an organization created in the aftermath of the September 11 terrorist attacks. Secondary trauma has been researched in first responders, nurses and physicians, mental healthcare workers, and children of traumatized parents.[30] *"A 2012 survey of 133 trauma surgeons, using a secondary stress trauma scale, found evidence of post-traumatic stress disorder in two-thirds of respondents."*[31] Learning that a relative or close friend was killed, injured or threatened with death or serious injury can put someone at risk for PTSD, according to the American Psychiatric Association's Diagnostic and Statistical Manual of Mental Disorders (DSM-5). People with PTSD may experience nightmares, hyper-vigilance, mood changes, emotional distress, and a loss of interest in their usual activities.[32] The effects on children, such as the young family members, friends, and school peers of those lost in the Sandy Hook Elementary, Stoneman Douglas and Columbine High School massacres, can have a lifelong impact if left untreated. Viewed as toxic stress, children can develop post-traumatic stress disorder that impacts brain development and physical health. Academic achievement, future professional success, and family stability are all negatively impacted as well.

Since the 2012 Sandy Hook massacre, there have been more than 400 school shootings in this country, reports the *New York Times*.[33] At the close of the 2019 calendar year, there had been 423 mass killings in this country, defined by the Justice Department as three or more deaths in a single event. This is the highest rate of mass killings since the database was established in the 1970s. The future of our children, and our society at large, is at risk.

I have firsthand experience with the impact of vicarious trauma caused by gun violence. My first exposure to vicarious and secondary trauma took place in the late 1980s through the early 2000s, when working in Lockerbie and then in New York, first in the wake of the TWA Flight #800 explosion and then immediately after the 9/11 attacks. But more recently, and continuing even as I write this book, I'm working with the first and last responders of the Route 91 Harvest Music Festival massacre on the Las Vegas Strip, which took place on October 1, 2017.

Ironically, the morning after the shooting took place, I was scheduled to depart my home in Las Vegas on an early flight to Dallas to conduct training at American Airlines' well-established Critical Incident Response Program. I was asleep by 10:00 p.m. the night before when the shooting began, and I was awakened by a colleague who informed me that numerous people had just been killed and injured on the Las Vegas Strip. I was conflicted about whether to leave for Dallas or stay to help the first responders. The city had not yet called to request my involvement. I honored my commitment to American Airlines. From Dallas, I was in contact with the coordinators for all jurisdictional fire departments in and surrounding Las Vegas. I was also in contact with the Police Employee Assistance Program (PEAP) and let them know that I would be available to assist them as soon as I returned home. I had full confidence in the first responders' ability to manage the situation on the Strip. I felt this way because I had trained them in the same techniques that had called me to Dallas.

I moved to Nevada from California in the fall of 2013 to run the chemical dependency treatment program at the Las Vegas Recovery Center. Within a few months of my arrival, I received a call from the Henderson Fire Department—about sixteen miles from Las Vegas—expressing an interest in Critical Incident Stress Management (CISM) training and consultation in setting up an integrated program for their department. This was my introduction to the extended Las Vegas community of first responders.

The training is comprised of pre-incident training and organization, appropriate and targeted interventions, and continuity of care. It is essentially psychological first aid. I conducted several training classes on CISM for Henderson and other fire departments throughout the area; various police department personnel also attended the training. By the time Stephen Paddock opened fire on the attendees of the music festival the night of October 1, 2017, Las Vegas had over 160 trained critical incident response volunteers at the ready to help their first responder peers—law enforcement officers, security officers, emergency medical technicians (EMTs), firefighters, and paramedics. After the shooting, I assisted these teams with debriefings.

Up to that point, the training had been provided to first responders but not to last responders. Last responders, comprised of coroners and medical examiners, are frequently omitted when city or county police or fire department decides to take up the critical incident response-training program. But I knew from my experiences in New York how valuable the training of coroners and medical examiners would be. When I asked the first responders in Las Vegas about this, I was assured the last responders had teams in place. But two weeks after the massacre, while attending a multi-agency meeting held at the coroner's office, it became evident that wasn't the case. My colleague, Stephanie Glover, and I worked with Clark County Coroner John Fudenberg and his staff (Clark County includes the cities of Las Vegas, Henderson, North Las Vegas, and Mesquite) in training a team on CISM. In the last couple of years, I have consulted with the Office of Chief Medical Examiner (OCME) of New York to develop a wellness program for the medical examiners' staff and presented at the International Association of Coroners and Medical Examiners Conference in 2018. Every occasion I have to speak publically, which is often, I promote the need for all mental health professionals who are in the business of responding to disasters to be cognizant of the coroner's offices and their specific needs.

The impact this massacre has had on my city still demands my availability today, three years later, as I continue to conduct CISM training. The festival was the deadliest mass shooting in modern US history: sixty people were murdered and nearly 870 more injured. As a result of this event, the federal government and states tightened some gun regulations, including the March 2019 federal ban on "bump stock" devices, which had helped Stephen Paddock, the Las Vegas gunman, shoot more people rapidly. Some states tightened gun laws, including passing "red flag" measures that allow a judge to order weapons removed from someone deemed a threat. In Nevada, lawmakers passed a measure that ended a two-year legal battle over a voter-approved initiative expanding gun buyer background checks to now include private gun sales and transfers. Democratic Nevada Governor Steve Sisolak called the measure a memorial to the music festival victims. And yet, nationwide, gun control advocates continue to be beyond frustrated at the lack of sensible legislation amidst the ongoing and seemingly endless violence.[34] Fourteen months after the massacre, in December of 2018, the Centers for Disease Control (CDC) released a report stating that gun deaths in this country were at a forty-year high[35]. The specific events and the statistics are astounding and lead to my conclusion that this is a national trauma.

Coping mechanisms and therapeutic models for the treatment of trauma and its offshoots of alcohol and drug abuse, depression, and PTSD are numerous and varied. Cultural immersion, as we saw in the story of the Alkali Lake people and Sam Schimmel, is one way through the pain and suffering. Counseling, peer support groups, meditation, and various psychotropic modalities, such as the supervised use of psychedelics, can all be effective pathways for others. Religious and spiritual faith can be healing for some, as well, especially when looked at in the context of current scientific findings. In the July 2, 2018 issue of *The New Yorker*, writer Nicola Twilley discusses the use of high-powered brain imaging to uncover neural patterns in her article "The Neuroscience of Pain." She interviewed and became a research subject of Dr. Irene Tracey at Oxford University's Nuffield Department of Clinical Neurosciences. Dr. Tracey is known as "the Queen of Pain." The results of one of Dr. Tracey's most fascinating experiments found that religious faith helps people cope with physical pain. While this has previously been an observation, breakthroughs in technology now allow researchers to watch images of the brain responding to pain and have learned that not all pain is experienced equally. Comparing the neurological responses of devout Catholics with those of atheists, Dr. Tracey found that when using advanced magnetic resonance imaging (MRI), the two groups had similar baseline experiences of pain, but when Catholics were shown a picture of the Virgin Mary while controlled pain was administered, they rated their discomfort nearly a point lower than the atheists did. When the volunteers were shown a secular painting, the two groups' responses were the same.

There are numerous areas in the brain that respond to pain, and on an MRI, all will light up when pain is felt. But one area, the dorsal posterior region of the insula, has been found to be consistently and highly active when the patient is experiencing pain. Dr. Tracey recently discovered that the blood flow to this part of the brain corresponds directly to the intensity of a prolonged painful experience. She calls the activity of this region of the insula a "biological benchmark for agony."

In addition to religious or spiritual faith being found to have a neurological response, Dr. Tracey also examined the effects of depression on pain perception. She found that several regions of the pain receptors in the brain were suppressed when she asked those subjects who suffered from depression to concentrate on a numerical task, like counting backward. Behavioral researchers have found that in depressives, distraction can reduce the perception of pain.

Depression is often a by-product of trauma, alcoholism, and drug use. Physical pain is also a by-product, not only of some specific types of traumas (such as domestic abuse and other forms of violence) but as a result of trauma being "stored" in the body, causing long-term and numerous diseases and disabilities. We may be more successful in helping those who suffer find sustainable recovery by reimagining our options for treatment. If we look to our cultural roots, our elders, and our connection with the land, sea and sky, the wounds caused by being ripped away from all that can be sutured, allowing us to begin to heal. If we also look at the newly emerging science and technology and accept that we can alter our own neurological responses to painful inputs, couldn't that, wouldn't that, potentially mean we are not forever defined by what others do to us? Instead, we would emerge phoenix-like from the depths of despair, loosened from those tethers of trauma, pain and addiction, and fly, free at last.

Chapter VII: The Woman in the Mirror

It all begins and ends in the same place ... We all come home eventually.

—Leon Uris

The view from my window seat as the plane descended was that of a falcon floating on the currents, gently swooping into a green velvet comforter of a valley. Green as emeralds, lush, verdant, and wide. Home.

The year was 2004, and I was returning to Ireland for my family's first reunion. I will forever be grateful to my dear cousin, Mary Ann, whose idea it was to get us all back together in our homeland. The far-flung family, comprised of my five siblings and thirty cousins, all gathered to meet in Glenbeigh, County Kerry, where my mother had been born, a mere thirteen kilometers from our birthplace of Killorglin.

Glenbeigh, known as "the jewel in the ring of Kerry," is surrounded by the Seefin Mountains and two rivers, the Caragh and the Behy, which run on either side of the town. This tiny village of fewer than three hundred back in 2004 is the flipped opposite of the landmarks in my hometown: I'd grown up by two mountains and a river, and here I was, nearly sixty years later, surrounded by two rivers and a mountain.

The tourist information for Glenbeigh markets the town as the "ideal holiday location." It doesn't take Freud or Jung or a PhD in psychology to tell you that family reunions are no holiday. But we all showed up, we all faced our fears—and there were many—and we came home.

"Home is wherever I'm with you."[36] We came to be with each other, which I've learned, is really the definition of home more than the geography of the place.

The composition of my family today is, blessedly, the same as it was in our childhood: we are five sisters and one brother. Not one of us stayed in Ireland; today, we are global citizens of Canada, England, Germany, Australia, Tunisia, and the United States. Not only did we leave the land of our birth, but we also left behind many of the customs our parents had embraced. None of us are nearly as religiously observant as our father had been. None of us partnered with anyone from our hometown as our parents had. Two of my sisters married German men; one sister married an Englishman; the other married a man from Northern Ireland, which may share the surname of our country of origin but is part of the UK. My brother married a woman from England. And then there was me; I was the only child of Molly and Tom who had married a man, Sean, from the Republic of Ireland.

My master's and doctorate degrees, which very possibly would not have been attained without Sean's support and encouragement, changed my life. I began to see where I came from, who I was, and why I was that person. Clinical terms designate families into functional and dysfunctional categories. Functional families usually provide an emotionally safe environment where parents work as a cooperative team, respect is honored, a resilient foundation is provided, privacy is recognized, people are held accountable, and apologies are offered when necessary. Functional families encourage their members to change and grow; individual differences are appreciated and respected. Children are encouraged to leave the safety of the nest and are welcomed back to that comfort and familiarity when they need or want nurturing. That was not the nest of my childhood.

In contrast, dysfunctional families are rife with conflict, abuse, and child neglect. There is also a denial of the covert or overt abusive behavior from one or both parents, leading the child to believe that it's their fault that they are beaten, neglected, or emotionally or sexually abused. There are usually inadequate boundaries in dysfunctional families, and privacy goes unrecognized. There can be a high level of jealousy among siblings: while they may express happiness for one another's success, they will also try to pull each other down. In dysfunctional families, the messages are not articulated but are quite clear nonetheless: you're not to talk about what's going on in the home, either among yourselves, with your parents, teachers, clergy, or your friends. Once put in place, the cone of silence is expected to be impregnable and remain ever so.

My family belongs in this latter category, and whether we acknowledged it or not, I think my siblings all knew this, explaining why we'd all left and why we all had fears about coming back and being together at that first reunion. There is an expression in Ireland: "You can take the man from the bog, but you can't take the bog from the man." This is a good metaphor for my family, possibly all families. While we all immigrated elsewhere, we each carry our own "bog" within us, the manifestation of our respective traumas, addictions, shame, and low self-esteem that haunt many of us to this day. One glaring symptom of our own transgenerational trauma is revealed in the dysfunction of my siblings' relationships with each other, which has been transmitted to the next generation. My nieces and nephews are not close to their cousins; they missed many years of knowing each other as a result of the maladjusted relationships between their parents. Members of my family went for extended periods of time, three decades in fact, without all gathering together. And when I was growing up, I wasn't close to my cousins either due to my parents' fractured relationships with their siblings. Looking backward and forward, this is a classic example of transgenerational dysfunction.

Transgenerational trauma cannot be healed if we continue to sweep it under the rug, denying its cause and continued existence. From outward appearances, my immediate family seems to have survived, even thrived, since our childhoods ended and we all got out of Ireland. To an outsider, we are well-adjusted, capable, competent, well-traveled, and accomplished in our different ways. Most of us are bilingual and have stressed the importance of education to our children and grandchildren, most of whom are now college graduates. The faces are all beaming in the family photo albums.

But there are a million miles between an outward and inward persona. All my siblings have suffered, to a varying degree, the common traits of our traumatic childhoods. We all live our lives under the overarching thunderhead of low self-esteem, anxiety, depression, and post-traumatic stress. Alcoholism is also a shared trait among us all and has spilled into the generation of my siblings' children, my nieces and nephews. To the best of my knowledge, I am the only one in recovery. My brother enjoys a very successful and long-term marriage (50 years!), but like me, several of my sisters are divorced, which is another sad hallmark of our adverse childhood experiences. We hadn't exactly had a strong model of a successful marriage held out to us by our parents, although as the years passed, their own relationship grew happier as the stressors of their earlier years faded. As a psychologist, I know that marriages are U-shaped, all fever and passion at the beginning, followed by a steep dip when challenges from various sources set in. My parents faced many obstacles: poverty, a large family, my father's lack of education, his alcoholism, his subsequent violent outbursts and physical abuse, and my mother's complacency. Over the years, as my siblings and I left home and started our own adult lives, both of my parents told me they had rekindled their love and had a kinder, more respectful relationship with one another until they were separated by death. But that was after we were gone and long after the damage to our childhoods had been exacted.

I also think that our immigration has played a significant role in our family dynamics: we're scattered across the globe, living our lives in six different countries. These geographical distances can't help but contribute to keeping us apart physically and emotionally. This begs the chicken and egg question: did we all disperse to the far corners of the world to consciously distance ourselves from the traumas of where we came from or did our childhood traumas predetermine the literal and figurative miles between us? We have spent many years, most of our lives, in fact, shoring up our fragmented selves where our private and public persona are split, concealing pain and loss while wanting so badly to be seen and to feel whole.

And so, it was this first reunion, in 2004, that brought us all back to Ireland for the first time in decades. In fact, all of us siblings hadn't been together since my parents' memorials, nearly thirty years earlier. That alone spoke volumes. I believe that being together earlier was too painful, our childhood memories too close to the surface and too easily triggered by one another. And because we were raised in a household where denial and suppression reigned, none of us had the language, the internal resources to know how to really talk to each other, to be honest and open about ourselves. Being vulnerable to others, especially within a damaged family, is terrifying. And yet, though we didn't know it at the time, it seems as if we had all heard the wisdom of Mother Teresa on the winds when she said, *"If you judge people, you have no time to love them."* We wanted to love each other; we did love each other. We just didn't know how to act upon that love.

I understand it takes awareness, commitment, and motivation to address and hopefully heal multigenerational trauma. At this time, at least, I'm not aware any such work has been undertaken by my siblings. We are not a chatty bunch, and the vulnerability of sharing our own painful, personal struggles with one another may never be overcome. And I see some of these same symptoms of our unspoken, unresolved family trauma—substance abuse, anxiety, and low self-esteem—playing out in my nieces and nephews. And yet I have an eternal hope that this younger generation will be more psychologically aware and do the work necessary to break this sad legacy we've given them. It is one of the reasons I've written my story. My hope for them flows from the fact that it is their generation, not mine or their parents,' that initiates the plans to keep these family reunions going.

Since 2004, we've continued celebrating family gatherings, sometimes in Ireland and sometimes in the US. Each time we come together, I feel an increased connection to my family as we all chip away at the defenses we've been expert at erecting. Each time we're together, we all walk through the door with our own strengths and weaknesses. We are all working on our own respective personal boundaries, non-existent in the dysfunctional family of our childhood and yet absolutely critical to becoming healthy adults. One way I have established my own boundaries is to always ask myself, prior to speaking to one of my relatives, especially in emotionally charged situations, "Is it true, is it kind, is it helpful?" These are simple but profound guidelines based, in part, on Buddhist principles. And if my answer is "No" to any one of those three questions, I keep my thoughts and opinions to myself. This has allowed me to not become entangled in family battles or to "triangulate," leveraging one person against another, which would damage these fragile bonds growing between us.

As the years have passed and the memories of our differences fade, these family reunions have allowed us, however cautiously, to grow closer. The time together has helped me accept, even honor, my own past and feel a sense of reverence for our ancestors. Families are the relationships you don't choose; they are inherited. I think that's what makes our familial relationships so fraught and yet so deeply poignant and impactful. Family members know us the best; family members don't know us at all. Family makes you feel safe; family is the seat of traumatic memories and nightmares. All of that is true and, in its own true way, beautiful and precious. In the end, being a family member is one of the hardest yet most heartfelt jobs any of us do in life.

All of us in this family enter our reunions a bit tattered around the edges and wary at the outset. But as the years have clicked by, we are letting go of our own "bogs;" we're laying down the past and building new memories of our own making, not the residual after-effects of who we were, where we came from, and what happened to us there. Our emotional healing occurs using storytelling, singing, playing music together, and most importantly, by being truly present with each other. I'm not naive enough to think these reunions are in lieu of personal therapy, but I do think these family gatherings have become, at least for me, integral to healing our own multigenerational trauma. In this way, my siblings and I have found ways to mend the damage of our childhoods by taking those scars, like threads, to weave new lives. The fabric of who we are will always show telltale signs, the little ragged pulls and snags of history, the dropped stitch of pain we choose not to remember. Time and experience mark us all, whether we come to comfortably wear those scars as proof of our survival or conceal them from the world and from ourselves. It is this woven new fabric of family that I hope my siblings and I will, in the end, safely wrap around the successive generations.

In December of 2018, as I was writing this chapter, an article was published in *The Daily Mail* titled "Lockerbie, then and now: how Scottish town has changed over 30 years." Time collapsed for a moment.

I read the story and viewed the many photographs juxtaposing Lockerbie today against those taken in the immediate aftermath of the explosion, just four days before Christmas, which rained pieces and parts of Pan Am Flight #103 onto that sleepy little town. The large crater, carved out of the earth by a wing section of the plane, displacing 1,500 tons of soil in its wake, has scabbed over and been filled in with grass and the asphalt of a new road laid down in the reconstruction of the neighborhood. The homes that were destroyed have been rebuilt; the trees that were torched have been replaced. What once was splintered and charred beyond recognition is now bucolic again. You'd have to look carefully to see what had happened thirty years ago; you'd have to intentionally seek out the small memorial at the spot where parts of the landing gear and a sixty-foot expanse of the fuselage had landed.

I read further. An article found on lockerbiecase.blogspot.com, writ-ten in October 2018, mentions how little in the town has changed:

> Other than the five memorials around town, there are few reminders of the tragedy. No plaques or signs mark many of the wreckage locations . . . Only different brickwork, an updated main road, and a memorial for the Sherwood Crescent victims hint at more . . . Residents say people from the United States and Scotland grieve differently: those from the U.S. do so publicly and the Scottish more privately . . . We don't talk about things like that. The town . . . I have to warn people that come here, it's not a disaster theme park . . .

These articles stopped my heart for a moment. I've come to realize that truth and falsehood can coexist in the same sentence; that ambiguity is more prevalent than cold fact. One of the captions under a photo in *The Daily Mail* piece read, "The forgotten remains of Pam Am flight 103, 30 years after the Lockerbie disaster lay in a scrap yard in Tattershall, Lincolnshire . . ." The aerial photo shows a pile of what looks like an active game of children's "pick-up-sticks," with heartbreakingly familiar dashes of blue thrown about, that signature blue of the Pan Am brand painted on the doomed carrier. The article goes on to say, "It is currently believed the scrap yard owners . . . are not allowed (by the government) to confirm its presence—nor explain why it is still there."

The falsehood in that caption is the word "forgotten," paired with the word "remains." How can something be forgotten and yet remain? "Forgotten remains" strikes me as a factual impossibility, a tragic misconception unwittingly promulgated right up there with telling children the dead are merely sleeping. Nothing in that, or any, disaster is ever forgotten. Not ever. The "remains," whether metal or bone, remain with us always. Forever. Like that crater gouged into the earth when the plane fell, in time, we scab the wound over. We plant new memories, and consciously or unconsciously, we might redesign our interior landscapes and alter the access roads to our hearts. But the history of the events that wound us never disappear. Not ever. Hiding that wound, like the scrap yard hidden in a wooded area outside of Lockerbie, and being told to keep it hidden shelters no one. You can lie, you can duck and dodge, you can deny its existence. You can repress; you can suppress. My personal life and those of my family members, my work, my patients and clients, and my academic learning have all taught me this, this one indisputable fact: you can do all that, but the thing is still there. The remains remain. And they will seek and eventually meet the light. Find relief in that; find your way free of it. We won't all be able to put all of that burden down, but in time and with care, making it a little lighter can be a good and gracious life to own. One day's burden is enough for one day.[37]

Epilogue

The heart breaks, and the heart opens.

On October 31, 2019, as I was finishing the manuscript of this book, my beautiful grandniece, my sister Maureen's granddaughter, Amelia, was found dead in Cambodia. She was a beautiful twenty-one-year-old woman who was much beloved by her large family. She had been traveling alone for the first time and was in Cambodia after having just visited her father, who lives in Vietnam.

I have spent my professional career counseling clients and addressing the public on trauma and loss. I have expertise. I have experience. I have hard-earned credentials demonstrating I know what I'm talking about, and I thought I knew what my clients were experiencing. But when my sister called me on October 26 to tell me Amelia was missing, I descended into an abyss that was, is, utterly unfamiliar in its depth, breadth, and darkness. Until tragedy strikes you personally, what we think we understand about heartbreak and permanent loss is similar to confusing the visible tip of the iceberg with the cause of what tore the *Titanic* to shreds.

The story of my life has been framed within my own experience, my placement in my family, and my family's placement in time and place. The traumas of my family have been, until Amelia, directly attributed to previous generations and that of my siblings and my own generation. We are now the elders, and with every passing year, we grow further from the source of that trauma. Our voices are becoming tremulous, our bodies are getting closer to the ground, and our eyesight, hearing, and thinking are less keen. This is the way it's supposed to be. This is natural, and this is right.

What is not natural and what is atrociously wrong is attending the memorial for your twenty-one-year-old lost darling girl. Now, with the loss of Amelia, my family traumas and their consequential effects will not end with us, with my siblings and me and our parents who came before. The hope I had at the start of writing this book was to show that transformation is possible, that hard personal work and an unflagging desire to be free from the damage of our past could lead to the cessation of multigenerational trauma. In the immediate aftermath of Amelia's death, my hope flagged, and I spiraled, thinking here's yet another trauma in our family, another devastation delivered. But as time has passed, I want to take that pain and shape it differently. I want to face the challenge of not repeating the mistakes of the past by transmitting this trauma to the next generation and the one after that. I want to know that I have learned something.

Amelia left behind a brother and three sisters, along with numerous cousins and countless friends. My generation is on the wane, and our family just ushered in a new trauma that will affect this younger generation, the children who carry forward not only our family name but also our sad family history. My generation needs to be accountable for what we have unwittingly passed down to them in terms of how we, their elders, dealt—or didn't—with our own hand-me-down traumas. Unless we break the pattern of repressing and silencing the painful things that happen to us and allow ourselves to drink it, medicate it, sleep it, or numb it away, that trauma will be transferred to our young ones. Unless we own those behaviors and understand their genesis, my fear is that Amelia's death will have been in vain.

Pain can be a great motivator for change; it can be an opportunity. My generation can help our children honor Amelia by making them aware of and helping them protect their own inherent strengths, the fulfillment of their own dreams, and their birthright to live whole, balanced lives. To do this, we need to encourage them to feel their loss and sorrow, help them form words around it, and speak to them about our own pain. We need to demonstrate and model to them what we, my brother and sisters, never learned from our own parents. This is how we will contain the effects of this family's tragedy and the children's individual responses to it so that they do not inadvertently, through silence and suppression, contaminate the family members not yet born, as our elders and we did. This is the only way we will ever break the cycle of multigenerational trauma.

Here in this epilogue to my life, all I can share with these lovely young people, my people, is my own experience over the arc of my life and what I am experiencing right now. My heart broke when Amelia died. This heart cannot be mended: when we suture a ruptured thing, we make it smaller. But I can make my broken heart an open heart. Open by allowing the grief to take up residence and not hurry its eviction. Open to feeling what I feel for as long as I feel it. Open to self-awareness that this pain is in perfect inverse proportion to the love I felt for Amelia, for my niece, who is her mother, and for Amelia's grandmother, who is my sister. The greater the love, the greater the pain. We don't always know just how deeply our love for others runs until they're gone, and in a moment, through the ringing of a phone or the pinging of a received text, we're struck to our knees, suddenly hollow and struggling to breathe.

When I could stand upright again, I saw that losing Amelia could bring something new to us, to our family. If you stand at the shoreline and something precious of yours falls into the water, the tide carries it away. And as you stand there troubling over what the sea just took from you, you will find it brought you a shell, now offered up at your feet. With each loss we experience, something can be gained. For me, attending Amelia's memorial in London brought me into contact with the now grown children and grandchildren of my siblings, some of whom I'd never met before, who had travelled to the memorial from distant places. Several of them reminded me of me, Maureen, Bridget, Eileen, Kathleen, and Patrick when we were young. Through the tragedy of losing one of our own, new ones arrived. The hole left behind in Amelia's absence will never be filled, but when talking with these younger generations, sharing stories, being asked questions about my past and asking them about their future dreams and ambitions, I felt something like comfort. It gives me perspective, hope, and a renewed sense of purpose and place. We are speechless in the pain of Amelia's death and yet have a new language between us. None of us went to her memorial thinking we'd somehow experience a sense of expansion by being together in letting her go. We loved Amelia, and when the tide pulled her away from us, she gave this large, far-flung, multigenerational and deeply wounded family a gift that shattered our hearts, providing us an opportunity to open up to the pain. This loss can propel us into the depth of the abyss, where we will surely drown, or we can choose to surface again, only altered, informed, transformed. Amelia gave us the gift of love that is now ours to pick up and carry forward.

Acknowledgements

You are going to feel like hell if you never write the stuff that is tugging on the sleeves in your heart--your stories, visions, memories, songs: your truth, your version of things, in your voice. That is really all you have to offer us, and it's why you were born.

—Anne Lamott

I am deeply grateful to my patients and fellow spiritual seekers whose courage in sharing their own painful stories has humbled and honored me and, in time and in turn, allowed me to tell my own story.

I am forever indebted to Dr. Tadao Ogura, my wonderful mentor and spiritual guide in New York throughout the 1980s, without whom I undoubtedly would still be flailing in free fall.

I'm eternally thankful to the late Doctor Garrett O'Conner, physician, psychiatrist, and the founding president of the Betty Ford Institute, and Doctor John McCann, the Medical Director of Pan American's medical department. Both gentlemen believed in me when I had no faith in myself.

As a woman now in the safe harbor of long-term sobriety, I am deeply appreciative of the recovery community and the inspiring friends I've made there over these last forty years.

Without the assistance of my co-author, Laurie R. Becker, my interior landscape would not have taken this exterior form. Over the course of writing this book together, we frequently experienced a "mind meld" where we seemed to intuit each other's thoughts, even finishing each other's sentences. The story is mine, the phrasing hers, the alchemy uniquely ours.

We both thank Kathy Ketcham for her significant contribution to the body of literature in the field of chemical dependencies and recovery, and for introducing me to Laurie. Additionally, and with heartfelt gratitude, Laurie thanks Kathy for her always wise, endlessly supportive, and loving input over the forty years of their most remarkable friendship.

We both thank Georgie Bambridge, my grandniece, and Hannah McGrath, Laurie's daughter, for their help in formatting the photo section of this book. The young ones teach their elders.

References

Chapter I

[1] Dan Buckley, Irish Examiner, "The silent terror that consumed so many" August 24, 2010

[2] Rainer Maria Rilke, Austrian novelist and poet, explaining his reason for declining psychological help

Chapter II

[3] Frank Abagnale, Catch Me If You Can 1980

[4] Bruce Handy, Vanity Fair, "Glamour With Altitude" May 28, 2014

[5] BBC Documentary, Come Fly With Me: The Story of Pan Am 2011

[6] CNN Travel, "Five ways Boeing's 747 jumbo jet changed travel" November 7, 2017

Chapter III

[7,10,11,12] Christine Negroni, Deadly Departure 2000

[8] The LA Times, "Law Helps Loved Ones of Air Crash Victims Cope" December 12, 2000

[9] New York Times front-page headlines, July 18, 1996

[13] Newsday, July 24, 1996

[14] National Transportation Safety Board Washington, D.C. 20594; Aircraft Accident Report In-flight Breakup Over the Atlantic Ocean, Trans World Airlines Flight 800, Boeing 747-131, N93119 Near East Moriches, New York July 17, 1996

[15] Petula Dvorak, The Washington Post, Sept 10, 2016

Chapter IV

[16] Fossion, P., Rejas, M., Servais, L., Pelc, I. & Hirsch, S. (2003) "Family approach with grandchildren of Holocaust survivors," American Journal of Psychotherapy

[17] David Brooks, "The Psych Approach" The New York Times, September 27, 2012

[18] World Health Organization, Geneva, Switzerland 2006, International Society for Prevention of Child Abuse and Neglect, "Preventing child maltreatment: a guide to taking action and generating evidence"

[19] Moffitt, Terrie E. (November 2013), The Klaus-Grawe 2012 Think Tank, "Childhood exposure to violence and lifelong health: Clinical intervention science and stress-biology research join forces." Development and Psychopathology. Cambridge University Press.

[20] ashwoodrecovery.com/blog/ptsd-substance-abuse-two-go-hand-hand/ Feb 28, 2017

[21] Clark, 2002; North et al, 1999

[22] Thich Nhat Hanh, Buddhist Monk, and activist

[23] Jennifer Bleyer, Psychology Today, "A Radical New Approach to Beating Addiction" May 2, 2017

Chapter V

[24] Judith Lewis Herman, Trauma and Recovery: The Aftermath of Violence - From Domestic Abuse to Political Terror

[25] Gloria Allred, discrimination attorney, feminist lawyer, and herself a victim of personal trauma, in Seeing Allred, a 2018 Netflix documentary

Chapter VI

[26] Oprah Winfrey

[27 & 28] Rebecca Hersher, "The Conflicting Educations of Sam Schimmel" aired on NPR's "All Things Considered" May 30th, 2018

[29] Lindsey Tanner, Chicago Tribune, "Las Vegas concert shooting puts many at risk for PTSD" Oct 04, 2017

[30] Cieslak R, Shoji K, Luszczynska A, Taylor S, Rogala A, Benight CC (September 2013). "Secondary trauma self-efficacy: concept and its measurement." Psychological Assessment; Kleim B, Westphal M (2011). "Mental health in first responders: A review and recommendation for prevention and intervention strategies." Traumatology; Beck CT (February 2011). "Secondary traumatic stress in nurses: a systematic review." Archives of Psychiatric Nursing; Lambert JE, Holzer J, Hasbun A (February 2014). "Association between parents' PTSD severity and children's psychological distress: a meta-analysis" Journal of Traumatic Stress.

[31] Tristram Korten, Modern Healthcare

[32] Ruben Castaneda, US News

[33] Sallie Jimenez, nurse.com, March 5th, 2018

[34] Ed Komenda, Reno Gazette Journal, "'You're always with us': Two years after Las Vegas shooting, community navigates loss," Oct. 1, 2019

[35] "The Hill" Dec 13, 2018

Chapter VII

[36] Alexander Ebert and Jade Allyson Castrinos, "Home" from their album Up From Below 2009

[37] The Bible, Matthew 6:34

About the Authors

Johanna O'Flaherty, PhD, is an expert in crisis management from a psychological perspective and a renowned expert in the field of trauma, addiction, and recovery. She was the vice president of Treatment Services at the Betty Ford Center from 2006 to 2013 before serving as CEO of the Las Vegas Recovery Center, Senior Fellow of Clinical Services, from 2013 to 2016. She is an Advanced Level Nationally Certified Addiction Specialist, a Certified Employee Assistance Professional (CEAP), and a Certified Trainer for Critical Incident Crisis Debriefing Programs. She received her Doctorate of Philosophy in Clinical Psychology from Pacifica Graduate Institute in California. In addition, Dr. O'Flaherty adds her forty years of personal recovery to her long list of accomplishments.

Dr. O'Flaherty developed and implemented Crisis Response Programs for Pan American World Airlines and TWA Airlines and has facilitated the training of Crisis Response Teams for several other airlines as well. In her role as Corporate Manager of Pan American Airways' Employee Assistance Programs (EAP), she was responsible for the oversight of bio-psycho-social-spiritual aspects of the 1988 Lockerbie disaster. This experience led her to become a pioneer in the aviation industry, organizing, training, and responding to aviation disasters and facilitating trauma processing, grief counseling, and critical incident stress debriefing. In 1988, she served as a volunteer with Catholic Charities in Calcutta, India, and presented educational programs on chemical dependency among young women. In 1996, she provided counseling services to the family members of 230 individuals who perished in New York on TWA Flight #800, the third-deadliest aviation accident in US history. In 2000, she received the FBI's Exceptional Service in the Public Interest award. In 2001, Dr. O'Flaherty was again called to New York to assist with counseling airline employees and facilitating the Crisis Response training for the New York City Transit Authority after the terrorist attacks of September 11. She has conducted critical incident response training for the FBI, first and last responders, and implemented training programs for hundreds of volunteers.

At the time of this writing, Dr. O'Flaherty is providing counseling to the first and last responders of the 2017 massacre at the Route 91 Harvest Music Festival on the Las Vegas Strip, at which 60 people were killed and another 869 injured. The incident is the deadliest mass shooting committed by an individual in the US and has reignited the debate over gun laws.

She is the author of two previous books: *The Correlation Between Trauma and Addiction* (2014) and *Daddy Goes to Meetings* (2015). She maintains a consulting practice and an active schedule as a keynote speaker in crisis management and addiction. Dr. O'Flaherty has been featured on CBS, ABC, NBC, and CNN, as well as several podcasts as an expert in her field.

Dr. O'Flaherty lives in Las Vegas, Nevada. She can be contacted through her website at johannahelps.com

Laurie R. Becker holds a BA in English Literature with an emphasis on creative writing from the University of Washington. She had more than a three-decade business career in Seattle, where she raised her two daughters. She now lives in Tucson and is a freelance writer and content editor of a published book, several scripts, and online content. She can be contacted at lrbecker03@gmail.com